# Model Railway Locomotive Building
## on the Cheap!

• SILVER LINK LIBRARY OF RAILWAY MODELLING •

# Model Railway Locomotive Building on the Cheap!

## An alternative to kit-building – how to convert ready-to-run models into unavailable classes or unusual variants

## K. Chadwick

Silver Link Publishing Ltd

First published in 2007

British Library Cataloguing in Publication Data

A catalogue record for this book is available from the British Library.

ISBN 978 1 85794 289 7

Silver Link Publishing Ltd
The Trundle
Ringstead Road
Great Addington
Kettering
Northants NN14 4BW

Tel/Fax: 01536 330588
email: sales@nostalgiacollection.com
Website: www.nostalgiacollection.com

Printed and bound in Great Britain

All photographs are by the author unless otherwise credited.

The author is grateful to the suppliers of parts used in the building of these locomotives, which were available at the time of writing.

Historical notes were compiled with the assistance of the RCTS 'Green Bible', *Locomotives of the LNER*.

A Silver Link book
from
*The* NOSTALGIA *Collection*

# PREFACE

When I returned to railway modelling in the early 1980s, after a 20-year absence, I found a situation that can best be described as 'Great Western overkill', with the LMS not far behind! The poor old LNER and Southern were very poorly represented in the ranks of ready-to-run locomotives. As these latter two railways were my main railway interest I had to resort to kits. Unfortunately, my own efforts at kit-building locomotives proved disastrous, and paying someone else to build locos for me proved expensive. Moreover, the kit-built locomotives were often unhappy negotiating tight-radius curves. So I began to rebuild existing ready-to-run locomotives, and the ensuing chapters are the result of my efforts – I hope they prove helpful to Southern and LNER modellers who are in the same situation as myself. Furthermore, who knows, if Messrs Hornby and Bachmann read this book maybe they will take note!

# CONTENTS

# USEFUL ADDRESSES

Dave Alexander Models
37 Glanton Road
North Shields
Northumberland
NE29 8LJ
Tel: 0191 257 6716

Bachmann Industries
    (Europe) Ltd
Service Department
Moat Way
Barwell
Leicestershire
LE9 8EY
Tel: 0870 751 9990

CGW Nameplates
Plas Cadfor
Llwyngwril
Gwynedd
Wales
LL37 2LA
Tel: 01341 250407

Classic Train and Motorbus
21B George Street
Royal Leamington Spa
Warwickshire
CV31 1HA
Tel: 01926 887499
(Suppliers of Jackson-Evans
detailing parts)

Comet Models
105 Mossfield Road
Kings Heath
Birmingham
B14 7JE
Tel: 0121 443 4000

Craftsman Models
1B St Johns
Warwick
CV34 4NE
Tel: 01926 402932

East Kent Models
89 High Street
Whitstable
Kent
CT5 1AY
Tel: 01227 770777

Fox Transfers
Cranberry End Studios
138 Main Street
Markfield
Leicestershire
LE67 9UX
Tel: 01530 242801

Alan Gibson
The Bungalow
Church Road
Lingwood
Norwich
Norfolk
NR13 4TR
Tel: 01603 715862

Guilplates
32 Wodeland Avenue
Guildford
Surrey
GU2 4JZ
Tel: 01483 565980 or
    563156

Hornby Hobbies Ltd
Customer Service
    Department
Westwood
Margate
Kent
CT9 4JX
Tel: 01843 233500

Jackson-Evans
4 Dartmouth Road
Wyken
Coventry
Warwickshire
CV2 3DQ
Tel: 0247 644 3010

Little Engines
201 Cheswick Drive
Gosforth
Newcastle-upon-Tyne
Northumberland
NE3 5DS
Tel: 0191 285 9873

Mainly Trains
Unit 1C
South Road Workshops
South Road
Watchet
West Somerset
TA23 0HF
Tel: 01984 634543
(Suppliers of almost
everything!)

Markits Ltd
PO Box 40
Watford
Herts
WD2 5TN

Slaters Plastikard Ltd
Royal Bank Building
Temple Road
Matlock Bath
Derbys
DE4 3PG
Tel: 01629 583993
(Suppliers of Plasticard,
Microstrip and other plastic
items, and 'Cavendish'
sprung buffers)

Modelmaster Transfers
PO Box 8560
Troon
Ayrshire
Scotland
KA10 6WX
Tel: 01292 314458

Modelspares Ltd
65 Burnley Road
Hapton
Near Burnley
Lancs
BB11 5QR
Tel: 01282 771109

South-Eastern Finecast
Glenn House
Hartfield Road
Forest Row
Sussex
RH18 5DEZ
Tel: 01342 824711

Springside Models
Unit 1
Silverhills Buildings
Decoy Industrial Estate
Newton Abbot
Devon
TQ12 5LZ
Tel: 01626 354972

W&T Manufacturing Ltd
Unit 19
Applins Farm Business
    Centre
Farrington
Dorset
DT11 8RA
Tel: 01747 811817

# Ex-LNER 'K4' 2-6-0 No 61994

**B**y the early 1930s the LNER was experiencing problems on the West Highland line, with trains of modern stock proving too heavy for the incumbent motive power ('D30s', 'D34s' and 'K2s'). So Gresley set his design team to producing a new 2-6-0 design for this work. The new design became Class 'K4', and the first loco (LNER No 3441 *Loch Long*) was introduced to service in January 1937. Over the following two years a further five locos were constructed. The design employed a boiler of 5ft 6in diameter, three cylinders, and driving wheels of 5ft 2in diameter. Originally the six locos were shared equally between Eastfield shed in Glasgow and Fort William, and spent almost all of their time working on the West Highland line, although there are reports of them appearing at Edinburgh, Perth, Aberdeen, Carlisle and even Tweedmouth on the North Eastern Region.

Their 5ft 6in-diameter boilers and 5ft 2in-diameter wheels gave them the power and surefootedness to master the gradients of the West Highland line, but their three-cylinder configuration did not agree with the multitude of tight curves on that line. On one occasion as a 'K4' was slogging up one of the gradients the middle big-end fractured and fell off! Maybe it was this occurrence that prompted Edward Thompson to rebuild No 3445 *MacCailin Mor* (later 61997) into a two-cylinder machine, the prototype of his 'K1' Class. After nationalisation production-series 'K1s' (augmented by some 'B1s') took over passenger services on the West Highland line, and the 'K4s' were relegated to freight trains only.

In 1959 the five remaining 'K4s' were all transferred to Thornton Junction shed in Fife, where they mostly worked freight trains with only occasional forays on passenger and excursion trains. All five locos were withdrawn from Thornton Junction during 1961, the last, No 61994 *The Great Marquess* being withdrawn in December of that year for preservation.

Until 1959 all locos ran with 3,500-gallon tenders, then in 1959 four of them (Nos 61993-96) were given 4,200-gallon straight-sided tenders (from withdrawn 'K3s'), with which they ran until final withdrawal. No 61994 was reunited with a 3,500-gallon tender after preservation. They were therefore not a very large class, and not very long-lived (only 24 years). They were also not very widespread, almost never being seen outside Scotland, but a model of one of these would be something different!

## Items required

Bachmann SR Class 'N' loco chassis; Hornby LNER Class 'B17' loco body; LNER 'Group Standard' straight-sided 3,500-gallon (or 4,200-gallon) tender (available from various sources – details in text); detailing parts as described in the text.

**Note** Although both Bachmann and Hornby do import some spare parts from China, the only way of obtaining a complete chassis is to 'cannibalise' a loco. So any shop/supplier that is willing to supply a Bachmann Class 'N' chassis is running the risk of being stuck with a loco body and tender that they are unable to sell (so who can blame them for being reluctant to do it!). I obtained the chassis for this project from the Bachmann Service and Spares Dept (it was from a model damaged in transit from China – this does occasionally happen and is another possible source). So potential loco-builders are advised to obtain the loco chassis before purchasing any of the other required parts.

*Above* The preserved LNER 'K4' No 3442 *The Great Marquess*, BR number 61994, repainted in LNER apple green livery and photographed at Nine Elms shed prior to working a rail-tour on 11 March 1967. *Frank Hornby*

*Below* The completed model. The nameplates are by Guilplates, with transfers by Fox, SMS and Modelmaster.

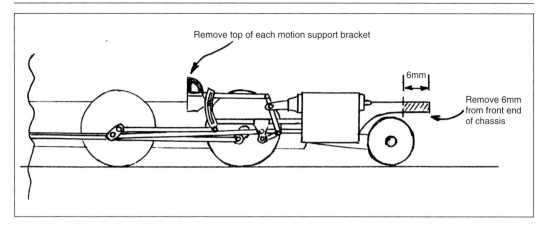

Figure 1: Modifications to Class 'N' loco chassis

## Stage 1: The loco chassis

Once you've obtained your loco chassis, it only requires two small modifications to enable it to fit the shortened 'B17' running-plate. These are the removal of the front 6mm of the chassis (over the pony-truck), and the tops of each motion support bracket (**Figure 1**). You will also need to fit a 12BA nut and bolt through a hole between the rear wheels to hold the rear of the chassis and the underframe tightly together (this job was previously performed by the body-fixing screw). With these jobs done the chassis is now complete.

## Stage 2: The Class 'B17' loco body

The Hornby 'B17' loco body comes in four separate parts: cab, boiler, smokebox, and running-plate.

Taking the running-plate first, we need to remove the protrusions on its underside (**Figure 2**). With this done we need to shorten the running-plate by 11mm, which is achieved by making two transverse saw-cuts (**Figure 3**), while at the same time removing part of the rear end of the running-plate to clear the Class 'N' motor-housing (also **Figure 3**). Next, clean up any rough edges with a file or emery-cloth and test-fit the rear portion of the running-plate over the Class 'N' motor-housing. If it fits over the motor satisfactorily, glue the two parts of the running-plate together, reinforcing the join with a piece of paper glued over it (**Figures 4 and 5**). This paper also covers the slots in the running-plate intended for the 'B17' driving wheels. Then drill a 2mm-diameter hole through the running-plate 2mm to the rear of the large hole (**Figure 3**) to align with a 12BA hole through the Class 'N' loco chassis; a 12BA nut and bolt passed through the two holes will fasten the body and chassis together.

We now turn our attention to the 'B17' cab. First, using a hacksaw or craft-knife, remove the protrusions from the cab front, then remove the

Figure 2: Modifications to underside of 'B17' running-plate

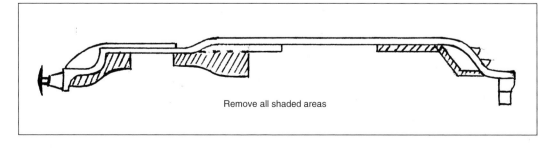

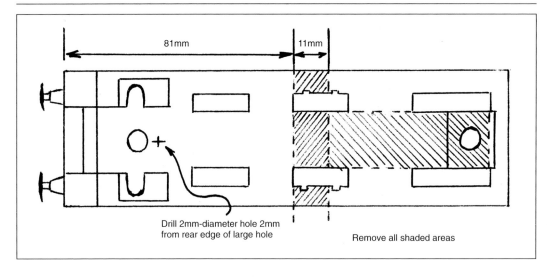

Figure 3: Further modifications to 'B17' running-plate

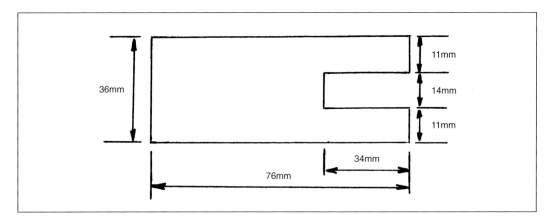

Figure 4: Dimensions of paper used to reinforce joint between two sections of running-plate

*Below* The re-assembled running-plate, showing the piece of paper reinforcing the joint.

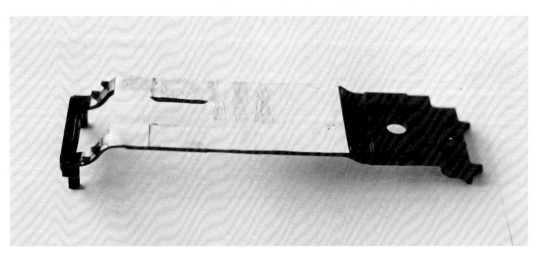

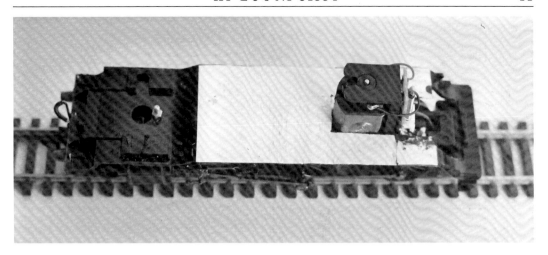

The chassis and running-plate fastened together (the 12BA nuts and bolts are visible between the cylinders and between the rear pair of wheels), with the Class 'N' motor-housing neatly accommodated.

locating hole for the body-fixing screw from the underside of the cab (**Figure 5**). Then cut out a piece of paper 33mm x 4mm and glue it to the bottom of the cab front to cover the wheel slots.

We now move on to the smokebox. Using a hacksaw or craft-knife, remove the chimney and file any residue flush. *Take care not to damage the snifting-valve.* Next file down the outside steam-pipes to a straight profile (**Figure 6**) (use photographs as a guide).

Note that No 61995 *Cameron of Lochiel* had an elbowed steam-pipe on the driver's side only – all the others were straight.

Next remove the smokebox door and its hinges. I find that the easiest way of doing this is to drill out the centre in stages, starting with a small drill (say 3mm diameter) and going up in stages to 10mm diameter – doing it in stages prevents the plastic from splitting/cracking. Then finish off with a craft-knife and file. Finally, with the craft-knife remove the regulator pipe (sometimes referred to as the vacuum ejector pipe) from the driver's side of the smokebox.

We now move on to the boiler. First we need to shorten it by 10mm by making two vertical

Figure 5: Modifications to cab

Figure 6: Modifications to smokebox

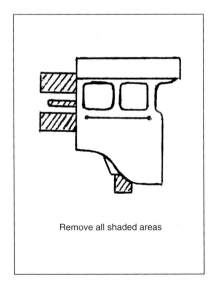

Remove all shaded areas

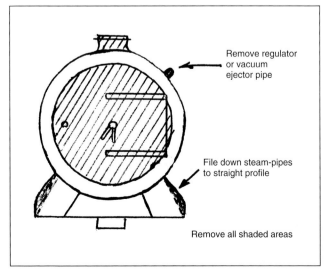

Remove regulator or vacuum ejector pipe

File down steam-pipes to straight profile

Remove all shaded areas

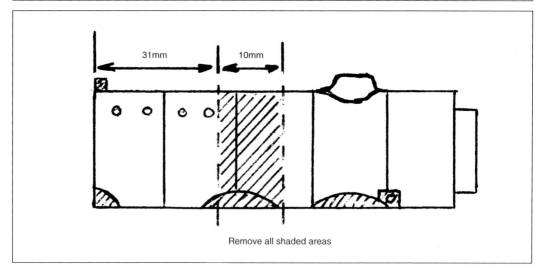

Remove all shaded areas

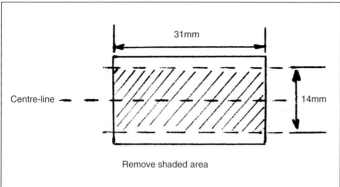

Remove shaded area

*Above* Figure 7: Modifications to 'B17' boiler

*Left* Figure 8: Modifications to underside of firebox

hacksaw cuts (**Figure 7**). File away any residue and remove the splashers. Then, again with a hacksaw, remove 14mm (7mm on either side of the centre-line) from the underside of the firebox (to clear the Class 'N' motor-housing) (**Figure 8**).

Next, with a craft-knife, remove the regulator pipe/vacuum ejector pipe from the two portions of the boiler. Finally, again with the craft-knife, remove the small lug from the top of the firebox that fits directly in front of the cab (**Figure 7**).

## Stage 3: Re-assembling the loco body

Unfortunately our model is going to have four boiler-bands, whereas the real thing has five! We'll have to put the difference down to 'modeller's licence', as the alternative would have been to have the third and fourth bands

ridiculously close together. As it stands, the 'B17' dome is in the correct position in relation to the 'K4' smokebox (and wheels, when we unite the body and chassis). It is also very close to the dimensions of the 'K4' dome, and although Dave Alexander produces a very good casting for a 'K4' dome, I would advise the retention of the Hornby 'B17' version. So we can now glue together the two portions of the boiler, making sure that they are straight and square, and put it aside to dry.

As regards the smokebox door, Dave Alexander produces a very good casting (from his 'K4' kit!). It comes already drilled to take a GN-style handrail and a Markits door-handle. Once you have fitted these two items, glue the smokebox door in position.

Now for the chimney. Again Dave Alexander produces a very good casting, and it needs fixing in the same position as its 'B17' predecessor.

With the chimney in place and correctly aligned, move on to the boiler.

With Milliput or similar, fill in any gaps in the joint between the two parts of the boiler, the gaps in the base caused by the removal of the splashers, and the holes in each side of the boiler and smokebox (for the fitting of the handrails – the 'K4' handrails were higher than those of the 'B17'). When the filler has set, file away any excess with emery-cloth, then unite the boiler with the smokebox.

Next, manufacture a regulator pipe/vacuum ejector pipe from a 90mm length of 1mm-diameter wire, and glue it to the left-hand side of the boiler in the position formerly occupied by the 'B17' handrail (use photographs as a guide). Hornby do (did!) a very good plastic moulding for one of these (intended for their 'A3'), and they are still available from Modelspares and East Kent Models. Then refit the 'B17' whistle and safety-valves.

The next task is to manufacture the boiler handrails. On the 'K4s' (as with most of Gresley's designs), these were not continuous and the rails on each side just curved around the front of the smokebox by approximately 6 inches (again, use photographs as a guide). I made mine from 104mm lengths of 0.7mm-diameter handrail wire supplied by Alan Gibson. When you have completed your handrails glue them to each side of the boiler – they need to be 3mm higher than their 'B17' predecessors (see photographs).

At this point it would be a good idea to paint the three parts of the body (black gloss – I used Humbrol). When the paint has dried, fit the front sand-box fillers. Dave Alexander produces castings for these (from his 'K4' kit!). As with the rest of his products, these castings are of very good quality, and they need to be glued to each side of the loco 35mm from the front buffer-beam, 8mm in from the edge of the running-plate. Next, fit the 'Wakefield' mechanical lubricators – castings for these are available from many manufacturers, and particularly good ones are produced by Dave Alexander, which come with separate brass wheels that look particularly good when assembled). These need to be glued to the right-hand running-plate 8mm in from its outside edge, at 44mm and 75mm from the front buffer-beam (use photographs as a guide).

Now drill three 1mm-diameter holes through the top of the running-plate just above the buffer-beam (to take the lamp-brackets) in the usual places, ie one above the front coupling and the others 3mm in from each outside edge. For the lamp-brackets themselves, I find that the Westward variety are particularly good.

In order for the firebox to clear the Class 'N' motor-housing we need to raise the top of the boiler and firebox by just 1mm. This is achieved by gluing two 33mm-long pieces of 1mm-square microstrip to each side of the base of the firebox. The smokebox is raised in a similar manner, by gluing two 17mm lengths of 1mm-square microstrip transversely across the front and rear edges of the smokebox saddle. When the glue has set, test the boiler for a straight and square fit and, if satisfactory, glue in place. Then glue the cab in place, ensuring a straight and square fit with the firebox.

Next glue a vacuum-pipe to the front of the buffer-beam (the Romford variety is particularly good). Then manufacture a reversing-rod from a piece of scrap brass or similar, 2mm wide and 46mm long, and glue it in place on the left-hand side of the loco (use photographs as a guide). Your loco is now ready for final painting and transfers.

The 'K4s' were all 'RA6' and, as far as I know, in the days of BR livery they all carried the 6MT power classification on their cab-sides.

## Stage 4: The tender

For most of their careers the 'K4s' were equipped with 3,500-gallon tenders, kits for these are available from DMR Products (a brass kit), South-Eastern Finecast (a white-metal body and etched-brass chassis), and Dave Alexander (all white-metal). In 1959 Nos 61993-96 acquired straight-sided 4,200-gallon tenders from withdrawn 'K3s', and ran with these tenders until final withdrawal in 1961. Kits for these tenders are available from DMR Products (an all-brass kit), South-Eastern Finecast (a white-metal body with etched-brass chassis), Dave Alexander (all white-metal), and Mainly Trains (employs a Bachmann plastic body and an etched-brass chassis). All of these kits required some proficiency with a soldering-iron, so those readers without the necessary skill may prefer to purchase a 'ready-to-run' Bachmann or Replica tender (from their 'B1' or 'K3'); at the time of writing these are available from Mainly Trains and East Kent Models. Note also that the purchase of one of these ready-to-run tenders will also save you the trouble of painting and lining-out.

If you decide to use a ready-to-run tender, you will need to remove the plastic drawbar and replace it with a simple piece of 1mm-diameter hand-rail wire bent to a squared U-shape. Glue one end under the tender drag-beam, while the other end simply hooks under the 'B17' cab – the length of the piece of wire will depend on your track radii. Also file away the mouldings on the front of the tender drag-beam (no one sees them and it will allow you to couple the loco and tender closer together).

The only photograph I have seen of a 'K4' with a 4,200-gallon tender is a front three-quarter view, so I don't know for sure whether the tenders had vacuum-tanks or not; however, if the tenders came from withdrawn 'K3s' there's a 90 per cent chance that they were so fitted. Very good white-metal castings for these are available from South-Eastern Finecast, and this casting goes on the *fireman's side* of the rear of the tender. Finally, if you decide to use a 4,200-

gallon tender you will need to give it a post-1956 BR crest (sometimes referred to as the 'ferret and dartboard').

## Stage 5: The finishing touches

We now need to do something about the yawning gap between the front of the loco-chassis and the buffer-beam. So, from card or Plasticard, manufacture new fronts for the frames (**Figure 9**) and glue them to the front of the chassis (do this job with the body attached).

Finally, a word or two about the nameplates. For most of their careers the 'K4' nameplates had black backgrounds. However, at some time during the late 1950s the Scottish Region authorities began to give their locomotive nameplates and numberplates light-blue backgrounds (that being the regional colour for the Scottish Region). If you want a light-blue nameplate set, Guilplates can supply these. The 'K4s' carried their nameplates on each side of the smokebox, and (with the exception of No 61993 *Loch Long*) the names were so long that the plates overlapped onto the boiler (see photographs as a guide).

So there we have it – a very useful and unusual addition to any ex-LNER layout.

Figure 9: Manufacture of new fronts for frames

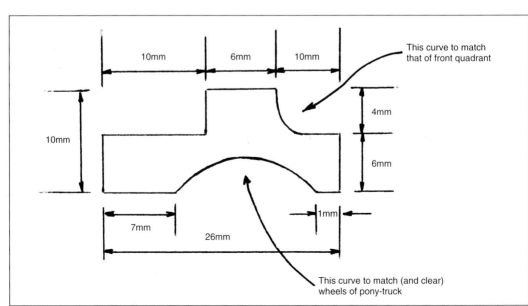

10mm   6mm   10mm

This curve to match that of front quadrant

4mm

10mm

6mm

7mm

26mm

1mm

This curve to match (and clear) wheels of pony-truck

# Ex-LNER 'K1' 2-6-0 Nos 61997 and 62057

In 1944 Edward Thompson decided to rebuild one of Gresley's 'K4' three-cylinder 'Moguls' with a shortened 100A ('B1') boiler and two outside cylinders. The loco chosen for rebuilding was LNER No 3445 *MacCailin Mor*, which emerged from Doncaster Works in its rebuilt form in December 1945. Throughout the following year the loco ran trials over many parts of the LNER system, and these were so successful that a further 70 locos were ordered from the North British Locomotive Co in July 1947, as Class 'K1'. These production-series locos were delivered during 1949 and 1950.

After its trials, the prototype loco returned to Scotland and worked alongside the 'K4s' on the West Highland line, and at nationalisation on 1 January 1948 it became No 61997. It spent the remainder of its life in Scotland and was withdrawn in 1961.

The production-series locos were numbered 62001-70 (the number 62000 was occupied by the 'CME's pet', a Class 'D3' 4-4-0 that was retained for hauling the CME's inspection saloon, and for some unknown reason the LNER hierarchy were averse to re-numbering it!). The 'K1s' were distributed to all three regions of the former LNER system, and could be seen at Stratford and King's Cross in the south, Mallaig, Glasgow, and Edinburgh in Scotland, and all points in between.

Withdrawals of the production-series locos began in December 1962 and continued steadily until September 1967 when the final four survivors (Nos 62011/45/50/60) were withdrawn from Tyne Dock (52H). No 62005 was put aside in August 1967 as a possible donor for a replacement boiler for the preserved 'K4' No 61994 *The Great Marquess*, and it survived in that capacity (stored at Neville Hill) until 1972, when it was purchased

for preservation (the boiler removal idea having been abandoned). Considering that it remained BR property until 1972 it must have the distinction of being the last main-line standard-gauge steam loco in BR ownership!

The 'K1s' were very popular engines and I haven't met anyone with a bad word to say about them. They were a fitting memorial to their designer, Edward Thompson, although most sources attribute the production-series locos to A. H. Peppercorn. Only minimal modifications were made to the original design – so surely Edward Thompson should get the credit for designing the whole class!

## Salient modelling points

No 61997 had a quadrant from running-plate to front buffer-beam whereas the production-series locos had a gap between them (to allow easier access to the valve-chests). Also No 61997 *did not* have electric headlamps, whereas all of the production-series locos did (or at least to begin with – a handful of locos had them removed towards the end of their careers). As regards smokebox doors, all of the production-series locos had the 'close-strapped' version (as fitted to the later 'B1s'). No 61997 had a 'normal' door (as fitted to the early 'B1s') from first rebuilding to the time of nationalisation. From nationalisation to approximately 1952 No 61997 also had a close-strapped door, then from 1952 to 1954 it ran with a close-strapped door, an extra handrail and an old-fashioned 'wheel and handle' fastening. From 1954 onwards it reverted to the same type of door as the production-series locos. So one of the production-series locos would be a worthwhile subject to model, and it would be at home on any ex-LNER layout.

*Above* 'K1' 2-6-0 No 61997 *MacCailin Mor* at Eastfield shed on 17 May 1953. *Frank Hornby*

*Below* The completed model of *MacCailin Mor*, which was made before Bachman introduced their Class 'N' 'Mogul', so used a 'V3' chassis and 'V2' tender. Making the body fit the chassis involved a lot of hard work, so the use of the 'N' chassis is by far the better option. The nameplates are by CGW.

*Above* One of the production-series 'K1s', No 62033, at Stratford shed on 7 June 1959. *Frank Hornby*

*Below* The completed model of 'K1' No 62057.

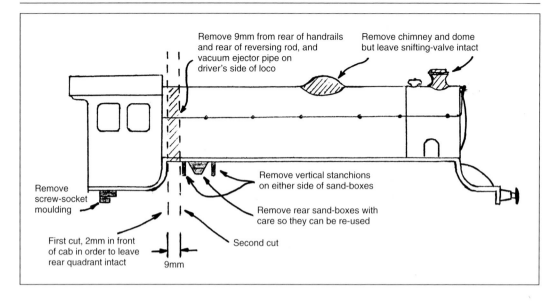

Figure 1: Modifications to 'B1' body

## Items required

Replica or Bachmann 'B1' loco body (if building No 61997 use early 'B1' body, ie without electric head-lamps; if building production-series loco use body of later 'B1', ie with electric headlamps and Stones generator already fitted); Replica or Bachmann complete 'B1' tender; Bachmann SR Class 'N' 'Mogul' loco chassis; detailing parts as described in the text.

See the note on page 7 regarding the sourcing of the Bachmann Class 'N' chassis by 'cannibalisation' of complete locos. Shops that have been known to 'cannibalise' Chinese-made locos in the past are The Hereford Model Centre and East Kent Models, and I obtained my Class 'N' loco chassis from the latter. So, as before, obtain your chassis first before buying any other parts. At the time of writing 'B1' loco bodies and tenders are available from Mainly Trains and East Kent Models.

## Stage 1: The loco body

First remove the whistle and safety-valves and put aside for safe-keeping. Then, with a hacksaw, remove the dome and the chimney while leaving the snifting-valve intact. Next, with a craft-knife, remove the rear sand-boxes from the

underside of the running-plate, together with the vertical stanchions on either side (**Figure 1**). Do this carefully and the sand-boxes can be re-used on the new model. Then, again with the craft-knife, remove the screw-socket moulding from the underside of the cab (**Figure 1** again). Next remove the chassis locating bracket from between the frames on the underside of the front quadrant (**Figure 2**).

Next we need to shorten the body by 9mm. Do this by making two vertical saw-cuts 9mm apart through the rear of the firebox. Note that

Figure 2: Modification to underside of front end of loco body

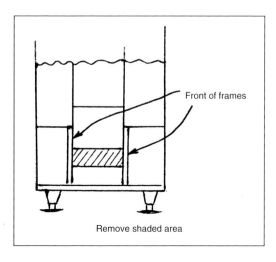

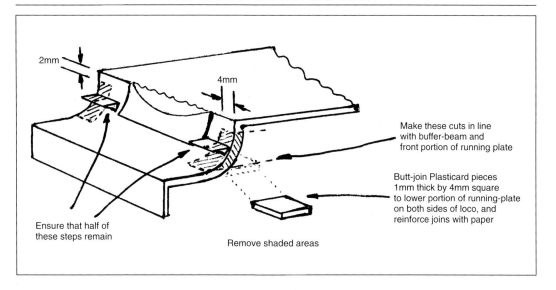

2mm

4mm

Make these cuts in line
with buffer-beam and
front portion of running plate

Butt-join Plasticard pieces
1mm thick by 4mm square
to lower portion of running-plate
on both sides of loco, and
reinforce joins with paper

Ensure that half of
these steps remain

Remove shaded areas

Figure 3: Modifications to front end of loco for production-series model only (boiler and fronts of frames omitted for clarity)

the rearmost cut is 2mm away from the front of the cab in order to preserve the rear quadrant. At the same time remove the rear 9mm of the boiler-side handrails with wire-cutters, together with the rear 9mm of the reversing-rod and the vacuum ejector pipe.

Next, *if constructing a model of one of the 'production-series' locos*, cut/file away part of the front quadrants (**Figure 3**). Then cut out two pieces of Plasticard, 1mm thick and 4mm square, and glue them to each side of the remaining lower portions of the running-plate (thus extending them by 4mm). Butt-join them, and reinforce with paper wrapped around top and bottom.

Next clean up the front of the cab and the rear of the boiler with a piece of emery-cloth, test-fit the two parts for a straight and square fit, then, when satisfied, glue the two parts together. Once the glue has set we can turn our attention to the top of the firebox. Having removed 9mm from the rear of the firebox, we are left with one safety-valve locating hole, which we can utilise for the whistle. Drill two 1mm-diameter holes for the safety-valves on the centre-line, 4mm apart with the rear one 4mm in front of the whistle. Then glue the whistle and safety-valves (re-using the originals from the 'B1') into these three holes.

We now move on to the chimney and dome.

There are a number of sources for these, including Markits Ltd (which produces both a chimney and a dome for a 'D49' that will fit the bill) and Dave Alexander, who produces suitable items (from his 'K4' kit). I used the Dave Alexander items. The new chimney and dome go in the same positions as their 'B1' predecessors.

Next, *but only if modelling a 'production-series' loco*, providing that your 'B1' body is one of the early versions without a Stones generator already fitted, a casting for this is available from Dave Alexander. Glue this casting on the right-hand running-plate at the side of the smokebox just in front of the steam-pipe (use photographs as a guide). Likewise, *if you are constructing a 'production-series' loco out of an early 'B1' body*, you will need a set of electric headlamps. These are also available from Dave Alexander. Use photographs as a guide for fitting them; note that the bottom-centre lamp-bracket has *two* lamps in front of it, and that the top lamp goes on top of the smokebox.

The production-series locos were fitted with AWS (Automatic Warning System) during the late 1950s/early '60s, and to model one so fitted you will need a 'vertically fitted AWS battery-box', available from Comet Models Ltd. This item goes on the underside of the cab in advance of the steps on the driver's (left-hand) side. You will also need an AWS 'Timing-reservoir' – a small cylinder on the left-hand running-plate immediately in advance of the cab and in front of the reversing-rod. The dimensions of the cylinder (in OO gauge) are 3mm diameter by 7mm long – I used a piece of plastic sprue from a Dapol kit. The AWS-fitted locos also had 'operating shoes' situated beneath the middle of the buffer-beam, and castings for these are commercially available, although you can't have one and an operational front coupling as well. So if you intend your loco to work trains tender-first you will have to dispense with this item (modeller's licence!). If you are using one of the later 'B1' bodies (with AWS fitted) it will have a 'vertically fitted AWS battery-box' on the right-hand side (the opposite side to the 'K1s'), so you will need to remove it with a craft-knife and re-fit it on the left-hand side.

Next glue the rear sand-boxes (from the 'B1') to the underside of the running-plate on each side of the loco, 5mm to the rear of the fourth boiler-band.

Now a word or two about the smokebox doors. The one on the Replica/Bachmann 'B1' appears to be part of the body moulding, so removing it would be a major operation, involving drilling out the centre then cutting/filing away the rest. . A close-strapped smokebox door is available from Dave Alexander (from his 'K4' kit). These could also be adapted to the varieties of door carried by No 61997. However, the Replica/Bachmann door bears a lot of fine detail – a good handle, a top lamp-bracket, and good straps. I decided to employ a bit of 'modeller's licence' and retain the original door; this might upset the 'rivet-counters', but it looks OK to me, and it also saved me a lot of hard work!

Next fit a small footstep to the smokebox door just below the lower hinge-strap, just off-centre to the driver's side of the centre-line. I obtained my step from a pack of 'Lamp-brackets and Steps' from Dart Castings Ltd. Finally fit a weight inside the front end of the boiler – I used a small AA-size battery held in place with Milliput. The body is now ready for painting and transfers – the livery carried in BR days was the mixed-traffic one. The locos were 'RA6', and had self-cleaning smokeboxes, ie they carried a small 'SC' plate fitted below the shedplate.

## Stage 2: The loco chassis

First, with a hacksaw, remove 3mm from the front of the chassis (**Figure 4**). Then cut out two pieces of 1mm-thick Plasticard, 11mm x 10mm, and glue these one on top of the other to the top surface of the chassis front (the front of the loco body will rest on these and the extra 2mm brings the body to the correct height). We now need to raise the level of the cylinder block by 2mm to reduce the gap between the cylinders and the running-plate. The cylinder-block is held in place by a 12BA self-tapping screw, which is easily removed. Cut out two pieces of 1mm-thick Plasticard, 18mm x 13mm, and drill a 2mm-diameter hole through each piece (**Figure 5**). Then glue them one on top of the other between the top of the chassis and the cylinder block while at the same time threading a 12BA bolt 12mm long through the ensemble. Then fit a 12BA nut to the end of the bolt and a spot of glue to prevent it working loose in traffic. Note that there must be no possibility of the cylinders themselves working loose while the loco is in traffic, so use plenty of glue together with the 12BA nut and bolt to make the assembly rock-solid!

We now turn our attention to the rear of the chassis. Just behind the motor you will find a 12BA hole passing through the chassis (there was formerly a self-tapping screw occupying this hole to hold the Class 'N' body to the chassis and underframe). Pass a 14mm-long 12BA nut and bolt through the hole to hold the rear of the underframe and chassis tightly together (add a spot of glue to the top of the nut to prevent it working loose in traffic). Next file away the raised portions at the top of each corner of the rear of the plastic underframe (**Figure 6**). Ensure that the remaining surfaces are level and square, for the rear of the body will rest on them.

When we place the body on the chassis we will find that there is a large gap between the top of the chassis and the underside of the body. In order to plug this gap take a 58mm-long piece of wood/balsa or square plastic tubing (Plastruct) 9.5mm square, cut out 2mm-deep slots to fit over the cylinder-block and the motion support bracket (**Figure 7**) and glue to the top of the chassis. Then cut out two pieces of paper 30mm

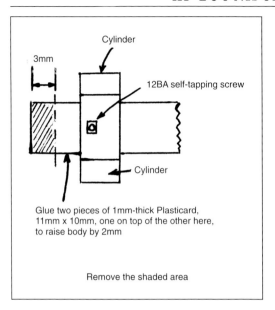

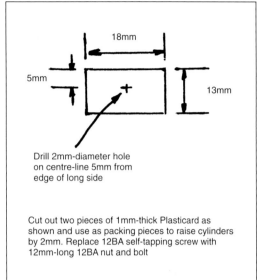

Drill 2mm-diameter hole
on centre-line 5mm from
edge of long side

Glue two pieces of 1mm-thick Plasticard,
11mm x 10mm, one on top of the other here,
to raise body by 2mm

Cut out two pieces of 1mm-thick Plasticard as
shown and use as packing pieces to raise cylinders
by 2mm. Replace 12BA self-tapping screw with
12mm-long 12BA nut and bolt

Remove the shaded area

*Above* Figure 4: Modifications to front of loco chassis (wheels omitted for clarity)

*Above right* Figure 5: Manufacture of cylinder block packing pieces

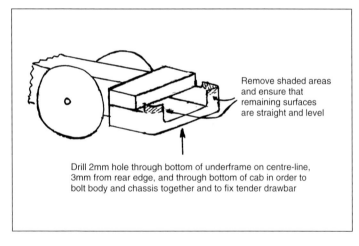

Remove shaded areas
and ensure that
remaining surfaces
are straight and level

Drill 2mm hole through bottom of underframe on centre-line,
3mm from rear edge, and through bottom of cab in order to
bolt body and chassis together and to fix tender drawbar

*Right* Figure 6: Modification of rear of loco chassis (motor omitted for clarity)

x 15mm to conceal the motor. It is a good idea to paint the paper black before fitting to the chassis (ever tried applying paint through the spokes of driving wheels?). When the paint has dried, glue the pieces of paper to the chassis between the centre and rear driving wheels on each side of the loco, thus concealing the motor below running-plate level (also **Figure 7**).

Finally, drill a 2mm-diameter hole through the rear of the plastic underframe on the centre-line 3mm from the rear edge – do this with the body in place on the chassis and continue the hole through the floor of the cab. This hole will now take a 12BA nut and bolt to hold the body and chassis together (this bolt can also be used for fitting the tender drawbar). With this done

all that remains to be done is the painting (black) of the balsa/wood/square plastic tubing that was added to the top of the chassis.

## Stage 3: The tender

At the time of writing, complete Replica and Bachmann 'B1' tenders are still obtainable from Mainly Trains and East Kent Models. If you use one of these, the only modification required is the replacement of the drawbar; however, if you file away all of the moulded detail from the drag-beam (when the loco and tender are coupled together no one sees it anyway) you can couple the loco and tender closer together. As regards a new drawbar, I made mine out of a piece of scrap

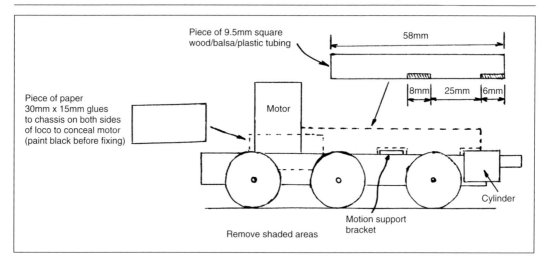

Piece of 9.5mm square wood/balsa/plastic tubing

58mm

8mm   25mm   6mm

Piece of paper 30mm x 15mm glues to chassis on both sides of loco to conceal motor (paint black before fixing)

Motor

Cylinder

Motion support bracket

Remove shaded areas

*Above* Figure 7: Filling gap between chassis and body and concealing motor (motion omitted for clarity)

*Right* The Class 'N' chassis after modification. The 12BA nuts and bolts are just visible at each end of the chassis. Note also the square plastic tubing, and the pieces of paper covering the bottom of the motor.

brass attached to the loco by the 12BA nut and bolt that holds the rear of the body and chassis together. The dimensions of the new drawbar will depend on the radii of your layout (so trial and error!). However, *if you are constructing a model of No 61997* this loco spent all its life coupled to a 3,500-gallon tender, which had a slightly different body, a wheelbase 6 inches shorter than the 'B1' tender, and a difference of 21 inches in overall length. Dave Alexander produces a white-metal kit for a 3,500-gallon tender (from his 'K4' kit); however, you could employ a bit of 'modeller's licence' and use a 'B1' tender. Glue a vacuum-tank to the rear right-hand corner (these are currently available from Modelspares and East Kent Models) and only a 'rivet-counter' will notice the difference!

## Stage 4: The finishing touches

Nameplates for No 61997 are available in OO gauge from Guilplates and Jackson-Evans, both of whom can also supply the relevant worksplates for the locomotive and the production-series models. CGW can also supply nameplates for No 61997, but are unable to supply worksplates.

Final bits of detail you could add, if modelling a production-series loco, are the cable-runs on the right-hand (fireman's) side of the loco: one from the cab to the Stones generator and the other from the generator to the top electric headlamp. First take a 95mm length of fine brass handrail wire, paint it black before fixing, then glue it to the boiler side to run from the front of the cab to the generator (curve it around the top of the steam-pipe). *Make sure you do this after you have fitted the boiler-band transfers.* Then take a 30mm length of the same handrail wire, bend it to the same curved profile as the smokebox, and glue it to the side of the smokebox to run from the generator to the top electric headlamp. When the glue has dried, paint the 'cable' black and your model is complete, adding a very useful locomotive to your stud.

# Ex-LNER 'D20' 4-4-0
# No 62343

In 1899 the North Eastern Railway introduced its Class 'R' 4-4-0s. They were designed by Wilson Worsdell and employed a boiler of 4ft 9in diameter, two inside cylinders and 6ft 10in driving wheels. A total of 60 locos were built, and they soon established a reputation for reliability and hard work that made them very popular with their crews. The locos were originally right-hand drive and dual-braked (vacuum and Westinghouse); the pump for the Westinghouse brake was situated on the right-hand side of the loco between the driving wheels and was partially hidden by the large combined splashers (see photographs). Vincent Raven began to fit superheaters to the class in 1912, and this resulted in them being fitted with longer smokeboxes. This work continued after the Grouping until the whole class had been so fitted in 1929. All 60 locos survived to become LNER Class 'D20' in 1923.

In 1936 one of the class (LNER No 2020, later BR No 62349) was rebuilt, completely changing its outward appearance. The Westinghouse brake equipment was removed and the loco was changed to left-hand drive. Three other members of the class (62360/71/75) were rebuilt to left-hand drive, but their outward appearance was left unaltered and their Westinghouse brake equipment was left in situ; these four rebuilt locos became LNER sub-class 'D20/2'.

The 'D20s' could be seen on all parts of the NER, and in pre-Grouping days (when the North Eastern worked all of the East Coast Main Line trains into and out of Edinburgh) a number of them were allocated to Haymarket. After the Grouping the 'D20s' were transferred back to North Eastern territory, although they still regularly worked across the border. During the 1920s they were often seen at King's Cross on excursions, but as larger and more modern locos became available their appearances grew less frequent. Members of the Botanic allocation regularly worked across the North Eastern's southern frontier into Doncaster until Botanic lost its last two (Nos 62381 and 62396) to Alnmouth in September 1957. Withdrawals began in January 1943 with LNER No 1147; after that withdrawals continued steadily, but 50 'D20s' survived to become BR property in 1948. The class finally became extinct in November 1957 when Nos 62381/95/96 were withdrawn from Alnmouth shed.

The 'D20s' lasted for 58 years and, though mainly confined to North Eastern territory, they were seen at King's Cross and Edinburgh in their early days. Therefore we have another long-lived class and, if your layout is set in North Eastern territory, one of these is a must!

## Items required

Hornby/Dapol/Mainline ex-LMS Class '2P' 4-4-0 loco; Hornby Class 'B17' loco cab; detailing parts as described in the text.

## Stage 1: The '2P' loco body

First of all separate the loco body from the chassis – they are held together by a screw beneath the cab and a brass screw at the front end, which also holds the bogie in place. Next (referring to **Figure 1**) remove the LMS-style pipework from the left-hand side of the smokebox. Also remove the cab – this is a separate moulding that is glued in place, but gentle coaxing with a penknife blade should remove it. With the cab gone it is now possible to remove the smokebox door – a gentle push

*Above*  Class 'D20/2' No 62375, one of four 'D20s' that were converted to left-hand drive, although their external appearance remained unaltered. It was photographed at Tweedmouth shed on 6 August 1955. *David Holmes*

*Below*  The completed model of 'D20' No 62343. The dome fitted to the model is from the Hornby 'E2' tank.

Figure 1: The '2P' loco body after
removal of indicated parts and cab

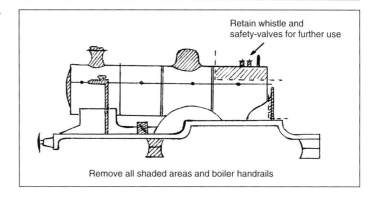

Retain whistle and
safety-valves for further use

Remove all shaded areas and boiler handrails

from behind with a pen or pencil should do the trick!

Next remove the whistle and safety-valves, retaining them for re-use. Then, with a hacksaw or craft-knife, remove the chimney and dome. Fill in the resultant holes with Milliput or similar and, when it has set, file away any residue flush with the boiler. Next remove the front steps, and as we will be doing a bit of work on the loco's front end later (lamp-brackets, 'piano-front' and new smokebox door) it may be an idea to remove the front vacuum-pipe to avoid damaging it.

As the 'D20s' all had continuous boiler handrails we shall have to remove the handrails of the '2P' (leave the knobs in place, however – we can re-employ them on the new model) – a penknife blade and a pair of pliers should do the trick. Next remove both mechanical lubricators with a craft-knife. Then remove the top of the Belpaire firebox with two horizontal saw-cuts just above the handrail-knobs on each side of the firebox, and a vertical saw-cut as near as possible

to the front of the firebox without damaging the adjacent boiler-band (**Figure 1**). Then clean up the edges of the saw-cuts with a file or emery-cloth.

Next file down the raised sections of the running-plate (including the quadrants) in readiness for fitting the combined splasher casings; the amount of material to be filed away will depend on the thickness of the material you intend to use for fabricating the casings.

## Stage 2: The 'B17' cab

First remove the protrusions from the front of the cab, then remove the floor, seats and firehole door in order to clear the driving wheels of the '2P' (**Figure 2**).

Next manufacture a new cab-front from card (**Figure 3**), and glue it over the original cab-front. When the glue has set, file away the parts of the cab that obscure the insides of the new round spectacles (**Figure 2**). Finally, using a

Figure 2: Modifications to 'B17' cab

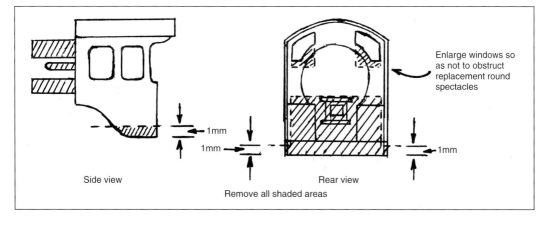

Enlarge windows so
as not to obstruct
replacement round
spectacles

1mm

1mm

1mm

Side view                              Rear view

Remove all shaded areas

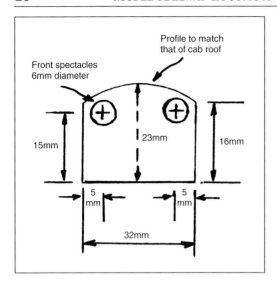

Figure 3: Dimensions of new cab front

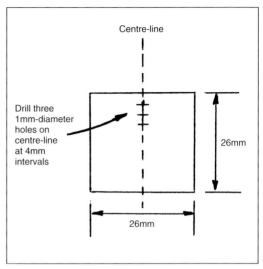

*Above* Figure 4: New top for firebox

craft-knife, remove 1mm from the bottom of each cab side-sheet.

## Stage 3: Re-assembling the loco body

First drill three 1mm-diameter holes through the running-plate above the buffer-beam (to take the lamp-brackets), one directly above the coupling and the other two 3mm in from each outside edge. Then drill another 1mm hole through the top of the smokebox 2mm from its leading edge, on the centre-line (to take the top lamp-bracket). Drill a further 1mm hole through the top of the smokebox, again on the centre-line, 3mm in advance of the first boiler-band (this hole will take the snifting-valve).

Next, from card, manufacture a new (round) top for the firebox, 26mm square. Make three 1mm-diameter holes (on the centre-line) at 4mm intervals to take the whistle and safety-valves (**Figure 4**). Bend the new firebox top to shape and glue in place (trimming if necessary), then cover the firebox with a piece of paper to hide the joins and the 'threepenny-bit effect' (**Figure 5**).

Now a word or two about the front frames. When originally built, the 'D20s' had frames very similar to those of the LMS '2Ps' (**Figure 6A**), with what is described as a 'concave front'. In 1912 Vincent Raven began to rebuild them

*Below* Figure 5: Paper cover for top of firebox

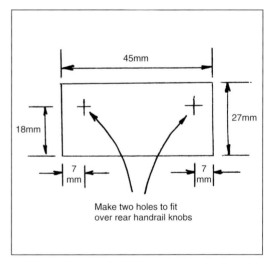

with a 'convex front' and deeper sections between the smokebox and leading splashers (**Figure 6B**). However, only 12 locos were so dealt with before the First World War brought more pressing demands on workshop capacity. The 12 locos were BR Nos 62342/47/49/52/53/60/63/66/89/96 and LNER Nos 2021/27 (the last two being withdrawn before national-isation). Therefore work from a photograph of the loco of your choice, manufacture the front frames as per Figure 6A or 6B, and glue them over the existing '2P' front frames ahead of the smokebox saddle, leaving the '2P' frames

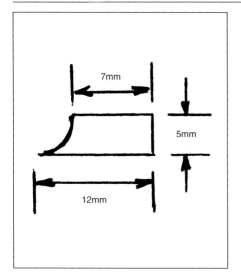

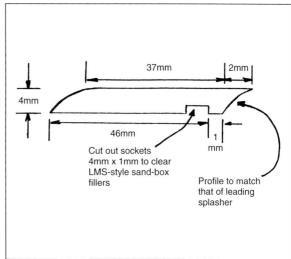

**Figure 6A:** Original Worsdell front frames as carried by the majority of 'D20s'

**Figure 6B:** 1912 Raven front frames as carried by 12 'D20s'

between the saddle and the splashers unaltered. Then manufacture a 'piano-front' from card 13mm x 10mm and glue in place between the front frames (to cover the piston tail-rods of the '2P').

Next glue the cab in place, ensuring a straight and square fit. Unfortunately the 'B17' cab, being longer than its LMS predecessor, overhangs the drag-beam by about 2mm. Camouflage this by gluing a 30mm length of 2.5mm-square microstrip between the 'B17' cab side-sheets (to represent the rear of the cab floor). At this point the more enterprising loco-builder may wish to add a new cab interior.

Next fit a Westinghouse pump to the right-hand side of the firebox. Castings for these are available from many sources. The deciding factor is the height of the casting – for the 'D20' it needs to be 15mm (so as not to obstruct the boiler handrail). Once you have fitted the pump (it goes exactly midway between the splashers on the right-hand side of the loco – use photographs as a guide) you can commence the manufacture of the new outside panels for the combined splashers, then glue the panels in place (**Figure 7**).

Next manufacture the tops of the splashers from card 59mm x 5mm, and cut a recess in one (to fit around the top of the Westinghouse

**Figure 7: Outside panels for combined splashers**

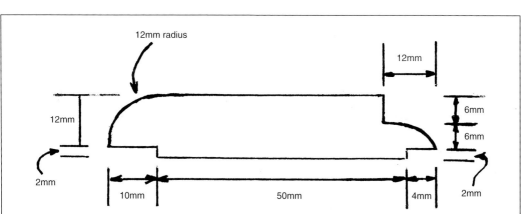

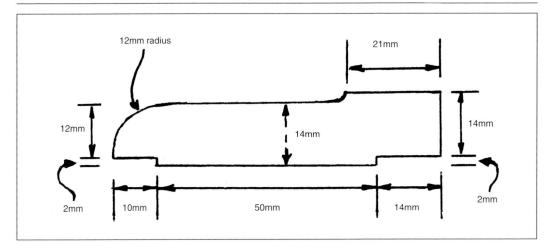

Figure 8: Paper covers for splashers and cab

pump); bend the leading ends to match the curves of the outside panels and glue in place. Then cut out two pieces of paper (**Figure 8**) and glue them to the outside surfaces of the cab and splashers, thus hiding the joins. To allow maintenance access to the Westinghouse pump the 'D20s' had access-holes cut into the right-hand splasher, covered with a circular hinged plate. To represent this plate cut out a card disc 6mm in diameter and glue it halfway up the side of the right-hand splasher in line with the pump.

One of the most characteristic features of the 'D20s' was the brass beading on the sides of the splashers. To replicate these cut out semi-circular pieces of thin Plasticard 2mm wide with an outside radius of 12mm (use photographs as a guide) and glue them to the sides of the splashers in line with each driving wheel. When the time comes for painting the model these will need to be painted with brass paint (for example No 54 in the Humbrol range). There were, however, a couple of locos that sustained collision damage during the 1940s: No 62343 had all four sets of beading removed, and No 62371 had the rear pair removed.

As regards reversing-rods, apart from the much-rebuilt No 62349 these were hardly visible – just an inverted 'L' jutting out from the front of the splasher (the right-hand one in the case of the right-hand drive locos Nos 62360/71/75). The required 'L' shape is easily manufactured from scrap brass (1mm wide) or 1mm-square

microstrip, or even (dare I say it) card (use photographs as a guide for its position).

Both the left-hand-drive and right-hand-drive locos had *one* mechanical lubricator situated on the right-hand running-plate in line with the centre of the rear bogie wheel. Castings for mechanical lubricators are available from various sources including Craftsman Models, South-Eastern Finecast and Dave Alexander; the last mentioned produces some very good ones that have a separate brass wheel which looks particularly good when assembled.

Next manufacture a regulator/vacuum ejector pipe from an 80mm length of 1mm diameter brass wire and glue it in place 4mm above the boiler handrail on either the left-hand or right-hand side of the loco (depending on the identity of your chosen model). Hornby do (or did) a very good plastic moulding for one of these pipes (for their 'A3'), and at the time of writing these are still available from Modelspares of Burnley and East Kent Models.

Next take a 62mm length of 0.45mm-diameter brass wire (supplied by Alan Gibson) and glue it to the left-hand side of the boiler to represent the pipe running from the Westinghouse pump to the side of the smokebox along the top of the splasher (use photographs as a guide).

Now a word about the smokebox doors. Approximately half of the locos retained their original North Eastern doors right through to withdrawal, while the remainder were fitted by

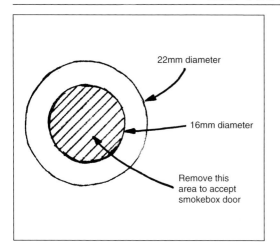

Figure 9: New smokebox front

the LNER with doors of a larger diameter (refer to photographs yet again). A very good white-metal casting for the original North Eastern-pattern door is available from Dave Alexander (from his 'J21' kit). It comes already drilled to take a Markits door-handle; once you've fitted the handle, in order to fit the door to the front of the smokebox manufacture a new smokebox front from card or Plasticard (**Figure 9**).

As regards the larger LNER-pattern door, a very good white-metal casting is available from South-Eastern Finecast (from their 'J38' and 'J39' kits). On my model I used a Hornby 8F smokebox door that I obtained from Modelspares of Burnley. When the holes for the handrail-knobs have been filled in, the 8F smokebox door is very close to the LNER version. Once you've fitted the smokebox door in place you can fit the lamp-brackets – the ones produced by Westward are particularly good.

Jackson-Evans produce some very nice etched-brass spectacle surrounds of the correct size for our model (6mm diameter) – part reference No 61 in their range. When glued in place they really enhance the appearance of the model! Next fit the safety-valves and whistle into the holes you made in the top of the firebox (I re-used the originals from the '2P'). Now fit the snifting-valve into the hole that you drilled for it in the top of the smokebox – very good castings for these are available from Markits Ltd, Mainly Trains and South-Eastern Finecast (from their 'J38' and 'J39' kits). I obtained a white-metal casting of the chimney from Little Engines Ltd (from their 'A7' kit), which is spot on for the 'D20'. Glue the chimney in place with its centre 10mm from the front edge of the smokebox.

As regards the dome, as with the smokebox doors the LNER began to replace the original North Eastern ones in the 1930s with what was described as 'a shorter, fatter type of dome'! But, as with the smokebox doors, not all of the locos were so treated and a fair number retained their original dome until withdrawal (yet again use photographs as a guide). Little Engines Ltd do a very good white-metal casting for the original North Eastern dome (from their 'A7' kit). Finding something for the later LNER-pattern dome proved somewhat harder, but eventually I discovered that the ex-LB&SCR 'E2' tank's dome was virtually spot on. A white-metal casting is available from South-Eastern Finecast, and (at the time of writing) a plastic moulding for the long-defunct Hornby 'E2' is available from East Kent Models. Whichever type of dome you use, position it with its centre 44mm from the leading edge of the smokebox.

Next return the vacuum brake-pipe of the '2P' to its original position on the buffer-beam; the model will only need one brake pipe (for the vacuum), as the pipe for the Westinghouse brakes was out of sight below the buffer-beam. Next fit the boiler handrail utilising the original '2P' handrail knobs. All the 'D20s' had continuous handrails that curved around the top of the smokebox door (use photographs as a guide). The handrails on my model are manufactured from a 206mm length of 0.45mm-diameter brass wire supplied by Alan Gibson.

We now turn our attention to the front steps. In common with other North Eastern classes, the 'D20s' had very elaborate front steps (see photographs). Possible sources for these items are Little Engines (from their 'A6' kit), and Autocomm Ltd (from their Nu-Cast 'F4' kit). However, if you are unable to obtain these castings you could manufacture your own steps from card (**Figure 10**). Then glue the front steps to the underside of each running-plate 36mm to the rear of the buffer-beam, ensuring that they do not interfere with the swing of the bogie. With this job done the loco body is complete.

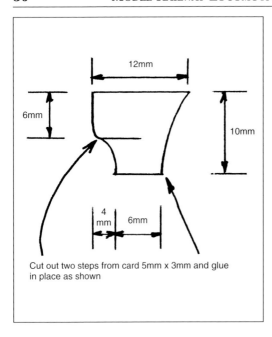

Cut out two steps from card 5mm x 3mm and glue in place as shown

Figure 10: New front steps

## Stage 4: The tender

When first introduced the 'D20s' were equipped with standard North Eastern tenders with a 12ft 8in wheelbase, while that of the '2P' variety is (or was) 13ft 0in, a difference in OO gauge of a little over 1mm. While the majority of the class ran with these original tenders right through to withdrawal, ten tenders were rebuilt between 1949 and 1950 because of badly corroded water-tanks. The chassis and frames were left unaltered but the bodies were rebuilt with straight sides, resulting in something almost identical to the LNER group standard 3,500-gallon tender. These ten rebuilt tenders were swapped around between locos, being recorded as having been attached to Nos 62341 (only 16 months), 62343 (seven months), 62348, 62351, 62353 (15 months), 62355, 62358, 62374, 62380, 62381, 62383, 62386, 62387, 62392 (18 months) and 62397.

From a modeller's point of view one of the rebuilt tenders would be the easier proposition; Dave Alexander produces a white-metal kit for the LNER group standard 3,500-gallon tender (from his 'K4' kit). South-Eastern Finecast also produce a white-metal kit for this tender (from their 'J38'/'J39' kit), while DMR Products Ltd

produce an etched-brass kit for one of these tenders. However, these kits don't come cheap, and the DMR kit would require some proficiency in soldering to assemble it. Another option (and probably the easiest) would be to use a Hornby 'D49'/'B17' tender body and shorten it by 6mm (**Figure 11**).

A further option would be to manufacture a new tender body from card or Plasticard to fit the dimensions of the '2P' tender chassis and power unit (use photographs and Figure 11 as a guide). White-metal castings for the tool-boxes, water-filler, water-dome and vacuum cylinder are available from the tender kit manufacturers previously mentioned.

Yet another option would be to remove the top 7mm from the '2P' tender sides and replace it with new tops manufactured from card or Plasticard (**Figure 12**), then add the white-metal castings for the LNER-pattern water-filler and vacuum cylinder. Finally, fill in the gaps between the new sides and the coal with Milliput or similar and cover with imitation coal.

If, however, the loco of your choice did not run with one of the rebuilt tenders, one of the original North Eastern 3,940-gallon tenders with four coal-rails will be required. Again, Dave Alexander produces a white-metal kit for one of these, while DMR Products Ltd produce an etched-brass kit. Both of these options would prove expensive, however, and the DMR kit would require some proficiency in soldering. It would, however, be possible to modify the '2P' tender body into something very close to the NER 3,940-gallon tender.

First remove the water-tank vents with a craft-knife, then drill out the LMS-style water-filler, fill or cover the resulting hole, and fit an LNER-pattern one; white-metal castings are available from Dave Alexander and South-Eastern Finecast. Then, from card, manufacture a new top for the tender (**Figure 13**), then glue it in place around the top of the tender.

Manufacture the four coal-rails from 1mm-diameter brass wire (available from Alan Gibson), bend them to shape and glue them to the newly made card top 1mm apart (yet again use photographs as a guide). Next drill two 1.5mm-diameter holes through the top of the

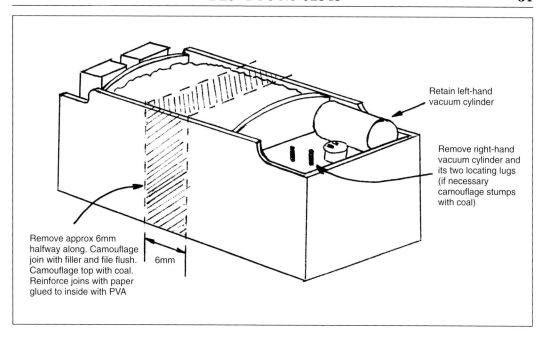

Retain left-hand vacuum cylinder

Remove right-hand vacuum cylinder and its two locating lugs (if necessary camouflage stumps with coal)

Remove approx 6mm halfway along. Camouflage join with filler and file flush. Camouflage top with coal. Reinforce joins with paper glued to inside with PVA

6mm

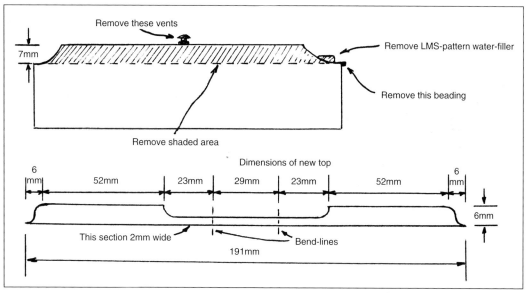

Remove these vents

7mm

Remove LMS-pattern water-filler

Remove this beading

Remove shaded area

Dimensions of new top

6 mm | 52mm | 23mm | 29mm | 23mm | 52mm | 6 mm

6mm

This section 2mm wide

Bend-lines

191mm

*Top* Figure 11: Modifications to Hornby 'D49' tender

*Above* Figure 12: Converting '2P' tender body into rebuilt 'D20' tender body

*Right* The completed NER tender body converted from the '2P' tender body.

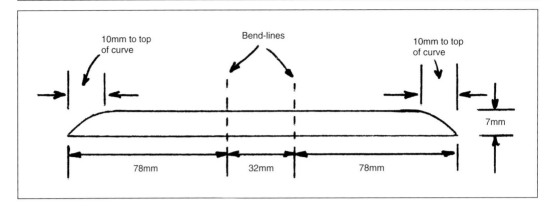

Figure 13: New top for NER 3,940-gallon tender

coal space 4mm from the leading coal partition and 2mm in from each side to take the tender vents – white-metal castings for LMS-pattern tender vents are available from Comet Models, Westward and Jackson-Evans and are very close to the required profile. With these fitted, the tender is complete.

## Stage 5: The loco chassis

Only one small modification needs to be made to the loco chassis: the large weight over the driving wheels is designed to fit inside the Belpaire firebox of the '2P', completely filling the space inside. Because we are changing the firebox to the round-topped variety we need to file a few millimetres off the top edge of the weight (**Figure 14**). When the completed body fits comfortably over the weight the chassis is complete and your model is ready for painting and transfers.

In BR days the livery carried was unlined black with brass beading on the splashers, although one loco (No 62343) had its beading removed due to collision damage. The route availability was 'RA6' and only the last two Botanic-based locos (Nos 62381 and 62396) received the later BR crest (referred to as the

'ferret and dartboard'). All the other BR-owned 'D20s' ended their days with the earlier 'lion and unicycle' crest.

The 'D20' makes yet another useful and interesting addition to any ex-LNER layout, and a very interesting and informative article on the class appeared in the January 1990 edition of *The Railway Magazine* written by a Mr T. Y. Nesider.

Figure 14: Modification to chassis weight

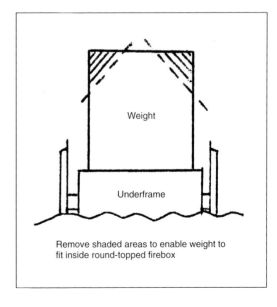

Weight

Underframe

Remove shaded areas to enable weight to fit inside round-topped firebox

# Ex-LNER 'D16/3' 4-4-0 No 62515

In the early 1930s the LNER rebuilt an ex-Great Eastern 'D16' 4-4-0 with a 'B17' boiler, and it was so successful that 90 locomotives were so dealt with. If you have a Great Eastern layout, one of these would be a very useful addition, so the subject of this 'rebuild' is a 'D16/3'.

## Items required

Hornby 'B12' loco body; Hornby 'B12' tender; Hornby 'Patriot' power unit; Hornby '2P' loco-chassis; two 8BA screws, one 4BA washer, and detailing parts as described in the text.

## Stage 1: The tender

First of all completely dismantle the 'B12' tender, and remove sufficient material from the tender floor/underframe to clear the motor-housing and gears of the power unit. Next drill a 2mm-diameter hole 12mm from the front of the tender frame (**Figure 1**). Now remove the wheels from the front (stepped end) of the 'Patriot' power unit and remove the 'step' with a hacksaw. When this is done, replace the front wheels, then remove the rear wheels and remove 3mm from the rear of the power unit. Test-fit the tender frame, and keep filing until the power unit fits inside the tender-frame, making sure that the rear wheels are clear of the coupling (**Figure 2**).

Next, with the power unit in place inside the tender frame, fit an 8BA screw into the hole that you have drilled through the frame to hold the frame and power unit together. Then fit the second 8BA screw, together with the 4BA washer, into the rear hole of the power unit. You will find that the washer overlaps the edge of the tender frame and holds the power unit and the frame firmly together (see the accompanying photograph). Next remove the screw/bolt housing from inside the tender body, then remove part of body underneath the footplate to allow the passage of wires from loco to power-unit (**Figure 3**).

*Left*  **Figure 1: Plan of Hornby 'B12' tender underframe**

*Below*  **The Hornby 'B12' tender frame ready for the fitting of the 'Patriot' power unit.**

Drill 2mm hole

12mm

Remove shaded area

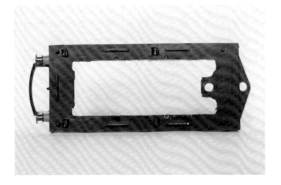

*Above* 'D16/3' 4-4-0 No 62567 at Bishopsgate Goods Station, London, on 6 September 1953 on an RCTS 'East Anglian' special train. *Frank Hornby*

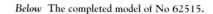

*Below* The completed model of No 62515.

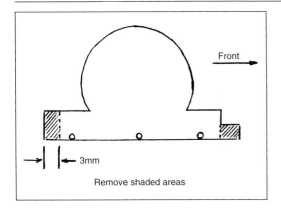

Figure 2: Modifications to Hornby 'Patriot' power unit (x.1075)

The Hornby 'B12' tender frame and 'Patriot' power unit assembled together. Note the 8BA screws and 4BA washer.

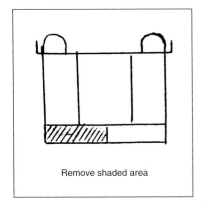

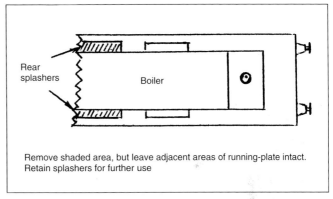

Figure 3: Front view of 'B12' tender

Figure 4: Removing the remaining splashers from the 'B12' body

## Stage 2: The 'B12' body

First remove the cab from the rest of the body with a hacksaw, then file the cab front flush. Next shorten the body by cutting through just to the rear of the fifth boiler-band. Be careful with the handrails – cut through them with wire-cutters. Clean up the rear end of the boiler with a file or emery-cloth and try it against the cab front. If it's a clean square fit, press on. Shortening the body will have taken away approximately one-third of the centre splasher, and the remaining two-thirds will need to be removed, while leaving intact the adjacent section of running-plate. *Do not damage or discard the splashers* (**Figure 4**).

Next remove the dome and the chimney, but *take care not to damage the snifting-valve*. Then, with a craft-knife, cut around the smokebox door

while leaving the outer rim of the smokebox (including the two handrail knobs) intact. We now come to the most difficult part of the operation – the removal of the body weight from inside the boiler. This requires a lot of coaxing, alternating with brute force, but it is possible, and is necessary to accommodate the chassis weight of the '2P'. Once the weight has been removed, offer the body to the '2P' chassis. You will find that the front splashers line up nicely with the leading driving wheels. Check that the 'slots' at the rear of the body (left by the removal of the 'B12' centre splashers) clear the rear driving wheels. If so, offer the cab to the rear of the body and chassis, checking especially for clearance of the driving wheels. If all is satisfactory, straight and square, glue the cab to the body. Make sure that both sides of the running-plate line up correctly.

When the glue has set, try the remains of the centre splashers in place on the running-plate in front of the cab. In order for the splashers to sit correctly over the rear pair of driving wheels they will need to be shortened by approximately 3mm. When you are satisfied with their clearances and appearance, glue them in place. Fill any gaps in the running-plate with filler. Likewise fill any gaps between the cab and the body with PVA adhesive (when the PVA dries it is clear and requires no painting).

When the filler has dried drill a 1mm-diameter hole on the centre-line of the boiler 2mm in front of the cab. Then drill another hole of the same diameter, again on the centre-line of the boiler, 4mm in front of the first hole. Finally drill a third 1mm hole on the boiler centre-line another 4mm in front of the second one. Into the holes place the whistle and safety-valves from the 'B12'. Then glue the dome in the same position as the 'B12' dome. I used a Dave Alexander 'K4' dome, but a 'D49' or 'B17' example would do just as well. Next glue an LNER standard 'flower-pot' chimney (available from many sources) in the same place as the 'B12' chimney. Next stick a Westinghouse pump (also available from many sources) on the right-hand side of the firebox aft of the fourth boiler-band (see photographs as a guide).

Now we come to the smokebox door. All the 'D16s' retained the peculiar Great Eastern smokebox door with the circular fitting rather than the conventional hinge-straps. The only source of one of these that I know of is South-Eastern Finecast (as used in their 'N7' kit). Glue the smokebox door in position just below the two handrail knobs on the smokebox front, then glue the smokebox door handle in place (again these are available from many sources – I used one of the Markits handles).

We now turn our attention to the front buffer-beam. All the 'D16s' were dual-braked, so two brake-pipes are required, one on either side of the coupling-hook (**Figure 5**).

Now you need to ask yourself whether you want your model to work trains tender-first? If the answer is no, remove the front coupling and think about guard-irons – the 'D15s' and 'D16s' had them fitted to the front buffer-beam (**Figure 5**). I made mine from thick cardboard 17mm

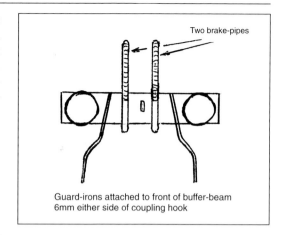

Two brake-pipes

Guard-irons attached to front of buffer-beam 6mm either side of coupling hook

Figure 5: Front buffer-beam

long and 2.5mm wide at the top tapering to 1mm at the bottom. I then bent them into a reverse curve and glued them to the buffer-beam 6mm on either side of the coupling-hook, with the wider end at the top (again see **Figure 5**).

# Stage 3: The finishing touches

Manufacture a tender drawbar from scrap brass or wire – its length will depend on your track radii and pointwork. Next solder the wires from the loco chassis to each of the terminals on the power unit, and give the loco a test-run. If you get nothing but short-circuits you'll have to de-solder the wires and swap them over. Then try again, and hopefully this time it will run OK. Once the loco is running you may notice that the rear driving wheels are reluctant to turn. I'm told by loco-kit builders that this is to do with balance – not enough weight over the rear driving wheels. All I can suggest is to put a metal weight inside the cab (there's nowhere else to put it!).

When the loco is running satisfactorily you can add the final touches – brake-pipes at the rear of the tender, fire-irons and numbers. Yet again be very careful when choosing an identity for your loco, for some members of the class retained the original valancing over the driving wheels (use photographs as a guide). A final tip: when ordering your 'B12' loco body and tender make sure that you get BR-liveried ones, otherwise the lining-out will be very hard work!

# Ex-LNER 'O4/6' 2-8-0
# No 63907

In 1918 the Great Central Railway introduced its Class '8M' 2-8-0 freight locomotives, designed by J. G. Robinson. They were intended to be an improvement on the highly successful Class '8K' introduced to service in 1911, with more than 600 examples having been built. The '8Ms' were, in fact, '8Ks' fitted with larger boilers (5ft 6in diameter compared to 5ft 0in). However, only 19 of the new class were built; the first 14 were given the same style of cab as the '8Ks', while the last five were given more modern side-window cabs (as fitted to the 'Large Director' Class 4-4-0s and many of the Great Central 4-6-0s).

The '8Ms' cannot have lived up to expectations, for in 1922 (just four years after their introduction) two members of the class were converted to Class '8K' (by replacing the boilers). At the 1923 Grouping the '8Ks' and '8Ms' became LNER Classes 'O4' and 'O5' respectively. The rebuilding to Class 'O4' continued under the LNER, albeit very slowly, the last 'O5' being rebuilt in January 1943 – more than 20 years to rebuild 19 locomotives!). The locos rebuilt from Class 'O5' became LNER sub-class 'O4/6'. The 14 locos with the original cabs were almost identical in outward appearance to older 'O4s', ie 'O4/1', 'O4/2' and 'O4/3', the only differences being in the design of the front spectacles, and all of the 'O4/6s' were vacuum-fitted (so a vacuum ejector pipe ran along the right-hand side of the boiler). The five locos fitted with side-window cabs retained them through to withdrawal.

In 1941 five 'O4/6s' were requisitioned by the War Department (together with 87 other 'O4s') and were sent to the Middle East. The remaining 14 locos survived to become BR property in 1948, the last example with side-window cab being withdrawn from service in 1962, while the very last example of Class 'O4/6' was withdrawn in June 1965.

Apart from their war service, the 'O4s' led unspectacular lives, hauling freight trains over the whole of the LNER system. In addition to their native Great Central territory they could be seen on Great Eastern metals, as well as in Scotland and all points in between. They were robust and reliable engines that seemed to thrive on neglect! Therefore every LNER layout should have at least one variety of 'O4'!

## Items required

Hornby '2800' loco body and Margate chassis (*not* Chinese) – it is also possible to use the LMS 8F chassis; Hornby 8F tender chassis (including power unit); Hornby 'B17' smokebox; 60mm length of 20mm-diameter pipe or broom handle; Hornby 'B17'/'D49' tender body; detailing parts as described in the text.

## Stage 1: The chassis

Whichever chassis you are using, first remove the 'firebox glow' assembly – because we are moving the cab further forward we have to dispense with this feature. This is the only modification required to the GWR '2800' chassis.

However, if you are using the 8F chassis, remove the cylinders and motion from the chassis block, and with a hacksaw remove the top half of the cylinders (the valve-chests) from the cylinder block. Then file down the remains of each cylinder into a more circular profile. Next cut out two pieces of paper 14mm x 25mm and glue them in place wrapped around each cylinder. When the glue has dried paint the cylinders black. Next,

*Above* 'O4/6' 2-8-0 No 63920 on empty stock at Drighlington on 9 August 1956. *David Holmes*

*Below* The completed model – a Mexborough 'Rod' in all its glory. I must admit that I never saw one as clean as this, but they must all have been 'ex-works' at some time in their careers!

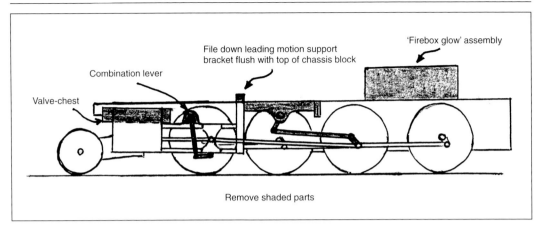

Valve-chest

Combination lever

File down leading motion support
bracket flush with top of chassis block

'Firebox glow' assembly

Remove shaded parts

*Above* Figure 1: Modifications to '8F' chassis

*Below* The modified '8F' chassis.

with a hacksaw, remove the combination lever from each crosshead and slide-bar assembly. Then remove the rearmost of the two motion support brackets, and file down the top of the leading motion support bracket until it is flush with the top of the chassis block. Now replace the slidebars, crossheads and connecting-rods to complete the chassis (**Figure 1**).

## Stage 2: The loco body

First of all remove the GWR whistle, buffers, boiler handrail and reversing-rod, then remove the struts connecting the underside of the smokebox to the buffer-beam. Next remove the boiler and smokebox by making a vertical cut, with a craft-knife or hacksaw, through the boiler at the point where it joins the firebox (take care not to damage the splashers). Then make a horizontal cut, level with the running-plate, through the base of the smokebox saddle. Cut also through the two circular boiler supports aft of the front splashers, again taking care not to damage the splashers. Finally, cut through the two pipes leading from the top-feed to the running-plate, and the boiler will come away.

Clean up any residue with a file or emery-cloth (**Figure 2**).

Next, *if you are using the 8F chassis*, part of the running-plate will have to be removed to accommodate the top of the motion support bracket, so cut or file a 4mm-wide socket in the underside of the running-plate (on both sides of the loco) 59mm from the front buffer-beam (again see **Figure 2**). Then remove the mysterious bracket from beneath the second splasher on the right-hand side of the loco. Next file or cut away the GWR numberplates from the cab sides. Remove the frames, steps and sand-boxes from the underside of the cab, *but leave the rear drag-beam intact* (**Figure 2** again). Retain the frames and sand-boxes for further use.

Now examine the underside of the cab and you will notice that the rear drag-beam has two square holes in it. When we shorten the body these will be utilised for holding the chassis locating lugs. However, first we need to remove the existing 'chassis location bracket' (**Figure 3**). A craft-knife is the best tool for this job, and when the bracket has been removed it is important to file away all of the residue to ensure that the body sits square on the chassis.

Figure 2: Modifications to '2800' loco body

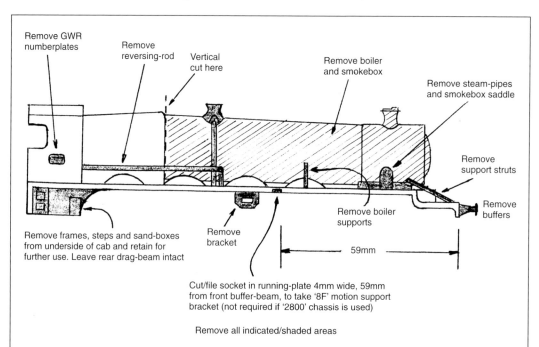

Remove GWR numberplates

Remove reversing-rod

Vertical cut here

Remove boiler and smokebox

Remove steam-pipes and smokebox saddle

Remove support struts

Remove buffers

Remove boiler supports

Remove frames, steps and sand-boxes from underside of cab and retain for further use. Leave rear drag-beam intact

Remove bracket

59mm

Cut/file socket in running-plate 4mm wide, 59mm from front buffer-beam, to take '8F' motion support bracket (not required if '2800' chassis is used)

Remove all indicated/shaded areas

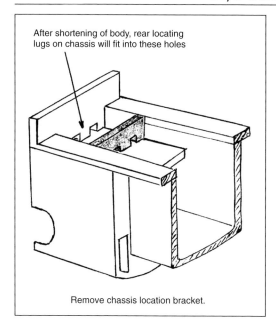

After shortening of body, rear locating lugs on chassis will fit into these holes

Remove chassis location bracket.

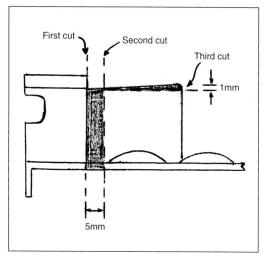

First cut    Second cut    Third cut
1mm
5mm

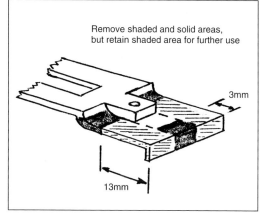

Remove shaded and solid areas, but retain shaded area for further use

3mm

13mm

*Above* Figure 3: Underside of '2800' cab

*Above right* Figure 4: Modifications to '2800' cab and firebox

*Right* Figure 5: Modifications to '2800' front buffer-beam

Next, with a hacksaw, remove the cab from the rest of the body, then make a second vertical cut 5mm ahead of the first (**Figure 4**). Then make a horizontal cut at the top of the firebox to get rid of its backward slope, starting at the front, 1mm below the top edge (also **Figure 4**).

Now we have to do something about the buffer-beam and the front portion of the running-plate – the 'O4s' had a straight running-plate at buffer-beam level, whereas that of the '2800' was slightly higher with a curved step to it, and this needs to be camouflaged in some way! First, with a hacksaw, remove the bufferstocks, then cut through each side of the running-plate horizontally at the top of each curve; take this cut as far as the raised section with the hole through it (**Figure 5**). Then make two further cuts through the front of the buffer-beam to link up with the first two cuts (again see **Figure 5**). This will remove the two outside portions of the buffer-beam. Now shorten these two outside portions to a length of 13mm (**Figure 5** again). Remove the front 3mm from the central section of the buffer-beam, and clean

up all the sawn edges with a file or emery-cloth, paying particular attention to the remaining leading edge of the running-plate – *this needs to be filed square*.

Now, from card or Plasticard, manufacture a new buffer-beam 33mm x 7mm, drill two 1.5mm-diameter holes on the horizontal centre-line 5mm from each outside edge (to take the buffers). Then drill a 1.5mm-diameter hole in the exact centre of the new buffer-beam (to take the coupling-hook). Now re-assemble the front end of the loco as shown in **Figure 6**. When the glue has dried, fill any gaps with Milliput or similar, including the large rectangular void in the centre.

Next manufacture a new top for the firebox from card or Plasticard (**Figure 7**). Drill three 1mm-diameter holes on the centre-line at 4mm intervals to take the whistle and safety-valves,

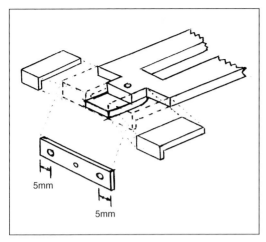

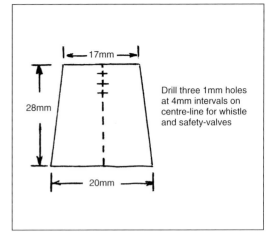

**Figure 6: Re-assembly of front buffer-beam**

**Figure 7: New top for firebox**

then glue the new piece in place on top of the firebox. When the glue has set, fill in the gaps around the top with Milliput or similar, then, when that has set, round off the top edges with a file or emery-cloth.

Now clean up the cab front and the rear of the firebox with a file or emery-cloth, and offer one to the other. When you have achieved a straight and square fit, glue the two parts together, and when the glue has dried fill any gaps with Milliput or similar. Then, from 1mm-square microstrip, cut two 35mm lengths to form the front and middle roof-ribs (the GWR cab roof already has ribs on the sides and rear); bend them to shape and glue them in place, on the leading edge of the roof and at exactly halfway (use photographs as a guide).

Next cut out a piece of card or Plasticard 5mm x 22mm and glue it to the tops of the third splashers in front of the firebox – this will support the rear of the boiler. Next, with a craft-knife, remove the mechanical lubricator from the right-hand running-plate of the '2800'.

Now make the combined splashers for the rear three pairs of wheels from card or Plasticard (**Figure 8**), and glue them in place over the existing splashers. Then make the combined splashers and sandboxes for the front driving wheels (**Figure 9**) and glue them in place over the existing splashers.

Now we must turn our attention to the boiler and smokebox. For my model I used the Hornby 'B17' smokebox (at the time of writing still

available from Modelspares of Burnley), together with a piece of 20mm-diameter plastic overflow pipe, 60mm long, for the boiler, with 1mm-wide strips of paper for the boiler-bands. The Belpaire-boilered 'O4s' had five boiler-bands; in OO gauge they will need to be 15mm apart. Next, from card or Plasticard, manufacture a 'support bracket' for the front of the boiler (**Figure 10**), and glue it to the leading inside edges of the front sand-boxes.

With the front boiler support bracket securely in place, offer the boiler to the front of the firebox for a straight and square fit. When satisfied, glue the boiler in place – the top of the boiler should be in line with the top of the firebox. While the glue is setting, check that the boiler is straight and square. When the glue has set, fill in any remaining gaps between boiler and firebox with Milliput or similar. When the filler has set, file flush as best you can, and cover the join with the fifth boiler-band (a 1mm wide strip of paper wrapped round the boiler).

Next, from a piece of scrap brass or microstrip manufacture a reversing-rod 2mm wide x 59mm long, and glue it to the right-hand side of the loco with the rear end 7mm above the running-plate and the leading end in line with the curved part of the splasher (use photographs as a guide). Then glue a 7mm-long piece of 2mm-square microstrip to the leading edge of the cab in front of the reversing-rod (again use photographs as a guide).

Next we turn our attention to the 'B17' smokebox. With a craft-knife remove the vacuum ejector pipe and the steam-pipes, then

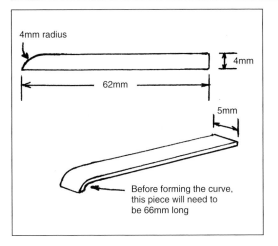

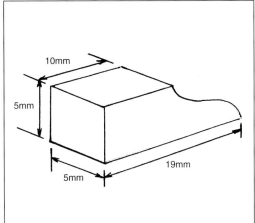

*Above* Figure 8: Combined splashers for rear three pairs of wheels

*Above right* Figure 9: New combined front splashers and sand-boxes for front pair of wheels

*Right* Figure 10: Front boiler support bracket

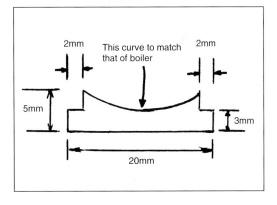

file down the sides of the saddle to a vertical profile (**Figure 11**). Then, again with the craft-knife, remove the smokebox door and its hinges. Next remove the chimney, making sure that you leave the snifting-valve undamaged. Finally clean up any residue with a file or emery-cloth.

Now a word or two about detailing parts. A Great Central smokebox door (with no hinge straps) can be obtained from Springside Models (from their Proscale ‘O4’ kit) and Craftsman Models (from their ‘A5’ kit) – on my model I used the latter. As regards domes, these are available from the two previously mentioned sources, together with DMR Products Ltd; on my model I used a Craftsman Models ‘early A5 dome’. As regards chimneys, these are available

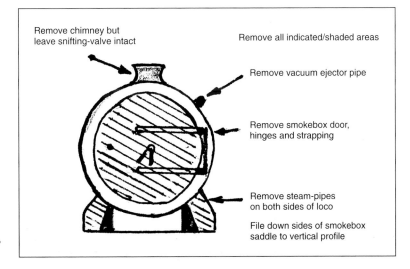

Figure 11: Modifications to ‘B17’ smokebox

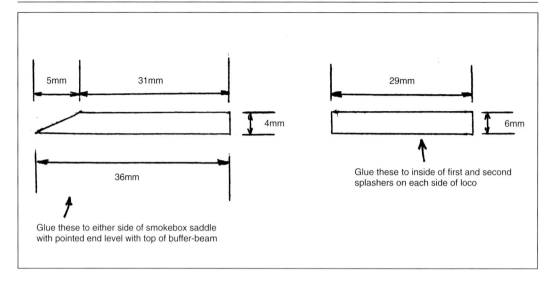

Figure 12: Making frame extensions

from the three previously mentioned sources, together with Markits and Cavendish Products; on my model I used the Cavendish version.

Glue the smokebox door in place, then the chimney (this goes in the same position as its 'B17' predecessor). Then glue the smokebox assembly into position, ensuring that it is straight and square with the boiler. When the glue has set, fill any remaining gaps with filler, and when that has set file flush, then cover the join with a 1mm wide strip of paper, representing the first boiler-band. Next glue the dome in position astride the third boiler-band, and check for alignment.

Next, from card or Plasticard, manufacture the frame extensions (**Figure 12**). Glue the shorter pair to the inside edges of the first and second splashers on each side of the loco (use photographs as a guide). Then glue the longer ones to the outside of the smokebox saddle on each side of the loco, with their pointed ends in line with the top of the buffer-beam (again use photographs a guide).

To make the 'piano-front', use two rectangular pieces of card or Plasticard 16mm x 5mm and glue these in place between the frame extensions directly in front of the smokebox door. Then take two 23mm lengths of 3mm-square microstrip and glue them to each side of the front frame extensions, with their rear ends butting against the front sand-boxes, and their

leading ends in line with the front of the smokebox. Then fit a Wakefield mechanical lubricator to the left-hand running-plate, immediately behind the leading splasher, backing on to the frame extension (use photographs as a guide).

Cut two 8mm lengths of 1mm-diameter handrail wire and glue the rail in place between the top and bottom edges of the cabside driver cut-outs. Next take the frames, sand-boxes and cab steps that were removed from the underside of the cab, cut away the remains of the GWR-style steps and file square (after the removal of the steps the frames should be approximately 15mm long). Then glue them to the underside of the cab, with the sand-boxes leading. Now glue a pair of cab steps to the rear of the two sand-boxes (cab steps are available from a multitude of sources).

Next fit the boiler handrails, whistle, Ross 'pop' safety-valves, lamp-brackets, coupling-hook, vacuum-pipe and, finally, Great Central-pattern oval buffers (these are available from Springside Models and Craftsman Models). The loco body is now complete and ready for painting; the livery in both LNER and BR days was unlined black.

## Stage 3: The tender

First, with a craft-knife, remove from the rear of the tender the water-filler and the four lugs (used

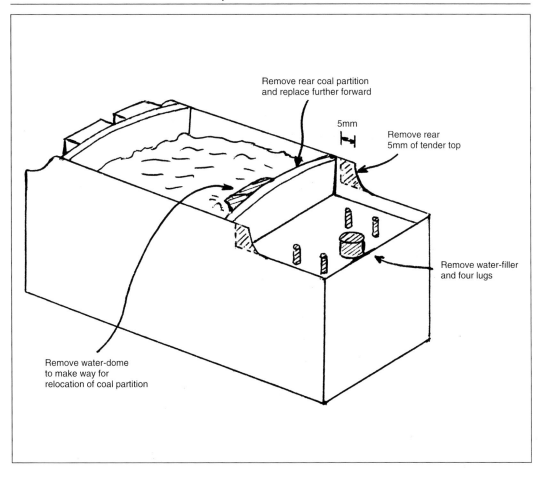

Remove rear coal partition
and replace further forward

5mm

Remove rear
5mm of tender top

Remove water-filler
and four lugs

Remove water-dome
to make way for
relocation of coal partition

Figure 13: Modifications to tender body

for locating the vacuum-tanks), and file flush as best you can without damaging the outside rim of the tender. Next remove the 'water dome' from the coal-space, then remove the rear coal partition (take care not to damage it as it will be re-used). Finally, remove the rear 5mm of the tender top (**Figure 13**).

Next glue the rear coal partition further forward (at the rear edge of the coal), then cut out a piece of paper 15mm square and glue it to the underside of the hole left by the removal of the water-dome. When the glue has set, camouflage the hole with imitation coal, and paint it black. Next cut out a piece of paper 30mm x 21mm and glue it over the top of the water tank.

Next make a pair of tender tops from card or Plasticard (**Figure 14**), and glue them to the tops of the 'D49' tender body to given the impression of stepped sides. Then manufacture a new water-filler (**Figure 15**) from card, Plasticard or even wood. Finally, glue a length of 1mm-square microstrip around the top back edge of the tender to make it resemble a flared top. The tender body is now complete and can be painted. The livery in both LNER and BR days was unlined black.

In order to make the LNER 'D49' tender body fit the LMS 8F tender frame, the six locating lugs on the tender frame need to be reduced in size (the LNER tender appears to be narrower than its LMS counterpart). Once this has been done, fit a pair of oval buffers and your model is complete!

A final observation: while this chapter describes construction of Class 'O4/6' No 63907, the same method of construction could be followed for a model of a Class 'O4/1', 'O4/2' or 'O4/3', utilising different boiler mountings, etc.

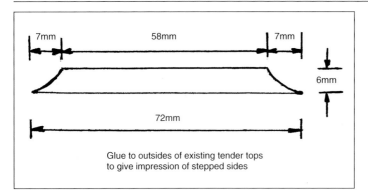

Figure 14: New tender tops

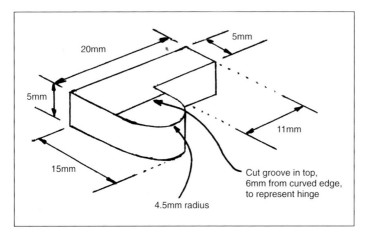

Figure 15: New tender water-filler

The completed tender for the 'O4/6'.

# Ex-LNER 'F4' 2-4-2T No 67155

In 1884 the Great Eastern Railway introduced its 'M15' Class of 2-4-2 tank locos designed by T. W. Worsdell. They proved to be poor machines – very bad riding and with a phenomenal fuel consumption that earned them the nickname 'Gobblers'. In 1885 Worsdell moved on to better things with the North Eastern Railway, and he was succeeded by James Holden, who halted the construction of 'M15s' in 1887 after 40 examples had been built. While new construction was concentrated on 0-4-4 tanks of Class 'S44' (LNER Class 'G4'), Holden 'tinkered' with an 'M15' at Stratford, trying to diagnose the problems. He found that the valve settings were wrong and that the loco was 'over-cylindered'. He therefore rebuilt the loco with smaller cylinders and replaced the original Joy valve-gear with Stephenson 'link motion'. These modifications did the trick, and the other 39 members of the class were similarly rebuilt.

Construction of new 'M15s' resumed in 1903 and continued until 1909, when the class total had reached 160 locomotives. Between 1911 and 1920 32 members of the class were rebuilt with new boilers of 180psi pressure, and these locos were classified by the Great Eastern as 'Class M15 rebuilt'. Ten members of Class 'M15' were withdrawn between 1913 and 1922, leaving 118 locos to become LNER Class 'F4' at the Grouping in 1923. Meanwhile, all 32 members of 'Class M15 rebuilt' survived to become LNER Class 'F5'.

At nationalisation on 1 January 1948 37 'F4s' and all 32 'F5s' survived to become BR property. While the 'F5s' spent all their careers stationed within the boundaries of the Eastern Region, the 'F4s' ventured further afield. In 1940/41 15 'F4s' were commandeered by the War Department for military service, and worked armoured trains in Kent, East Anglia and Scotland. In 1945 three 'F4s' were transferred to Dairycoates shed on the LNER's northern division, later becoming the North Eastern Region of BR, and remained there until withdrawal in 1951.

In 1931 three 'F4s' were transferred to Scotland, to be joined by a fourth example in 1948. These four locos spent most of their time in Scotland allocated to Kittybrewster shed (61A). Two of them were fitted with 'push and pull' equipment and 'cow-catchers' for working the Fraserburgh to St Combs branch. It was one of these four Scottish locos (No 67157) that had the distinction of being the last 'F4' to be withdrawn, in June 1956. Class 'F5' eventually became extinct in May 1958, with the withdrawal of Nos 67195 and 67212.

So here we have another large class (160 locos), and a long-lived one (more than 70 years). Members of Class 'F4' could be seen on the Eastern, North Eastern and Scottish Regions, and certainly no Great Eastern layout should be without one!

## Items required

Hornby or Dapol '1400' 0-4-2T loco; one pair of 15mm-diameter bogie-wheels; pony-truck from Hornby LNER 'Pacific' tender power unit (L.5136); detailing parts as described in the text.

## Stage 1: The chassis

First remove the front sand-boxes and the front coupling, then remove all the plastic underframe in front of the brake-gear of the leading wheels, but *leave the metal part of the underframe intact* (**Figure 1A**). File flush the raised parts of the exposed metal chassis block, then enlarge the

*Above* 'F4' 2-4-2T No 67187 (foreground) coupled to an 'F6' 2-4-2T at Lowestoft on 20 September 1953. *John Edgington*

*Below* The completed model of 'F4' No 67155 – a 'Gobbler' but certainly no turkey!

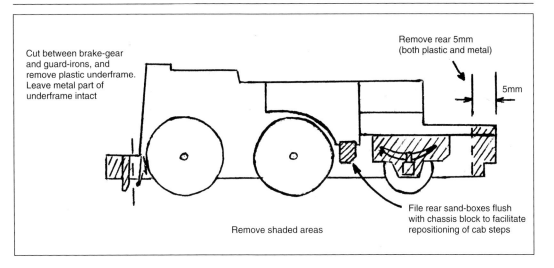

Cut between brake-gear and guard-irons, and remove plastic underframe. Leave metal part of underframe intact

Remove rear 5mm (both plastic and metal)

5mm

Remove shaded areas

File rear sand-boxes flush with chassis block to facilitate repositioning of cab steps

Figure 1A: Modification to the '1400' chassis

hole (use for securing the front sand-boxes) to 2mm or 8BA. Next, with a craft-knife, remove the outside frames from the rear wheels, then, with a hacksaw, remove the rear 5mm of the underframe and chassis block (**Figure 1A** again). Then clean up the sawn edges with a file.

Later, in Stage 2, we shall be lengthening the body to fit the chassis, and in doing this we shall end up with the cab steps directly over the rear sand-boxes. It is therefore a good idea at this point to file down the rear sand-boxes flush with the rest of the chassis block. The rear sand-boxes, of course, provided support for the rear of the body, so cut out a piece of wood or balsa

Figure 1B: New support for rear of body

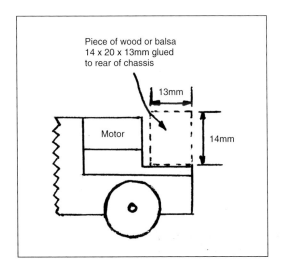

Piece of wood or balsa 14 x 20 x 13mm glued to rear of chassis

13mm

Motor

14mm

14mm x 20mm x 13mm, and glue it to the chassis directly behind the motor (**Figure 1B**). The rear of the body (coal-space) will now rest on this.

We now turn our attention to the pony-truck (L.5136). With a file or craft-knife remove the raised area around the pivot-hole. Fit the 15mm-diameter wheels in place, and attach the pony-truck to the chassis with a 10BA nut and bolt, passing through the hole at the front of the chassis. Check that the pony-truck swings satisfactorily and that the coupling is level. At this point it may be a good idea to add a small weight between the wheels of the pony-truck to increase stability.

Having removed the rear 5mm of the chassis, we need a new rear coupling, which can be attached either to the body (see Stage 2), or to the chassis, by drilling a 1mm-diameter hole transversely, in the horizontal plane, through the remains of the underframe, then fashioning the coupling from a length of 1mm-diameter wire bent to shape and passed through the hole in the underframe. With this done your chassis is now complete and you have created a 2-4-2.

## Stage 2: The body

First remove the handrail from the rear of the cab with a pen-knife blade, then remove the roof and rear of the cab. Then, with a craft-knife, remove the 'mushroom' vents from the top of the

The completed chassis. Note the 10BA nut and bolt and the pony-truck (L.5136). The piece of wood behind the motor supports the rear of the body.

tanks. Next remove the 'stump' of the GWR chimney and file flush with the top of the smokebox, then do the same with the GWR dome and fill the resultant hole with Milliput or similar. When the filler has set, file flush with the top of the boiler.

Next remove the top-feed, its associated pipework and the peculiar GWR pipe at the top

Figure 2: Modifications to '1400' cab and bunker

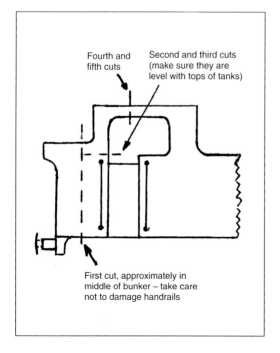

Fourth and fifth cuts

Second and third cuts (make sure they are level with tops of tanks)

First cut, approximately in middle of bunker – take care not to damage handrails

of the smokebox (between the chimney and the top-feed). Then, with a craft-knife, remove the splashers and tool-boxes. Next separate the boiler and smokebox from the rest of the body – they are held together by four lugs, two underneath the smokebox saddle and two under the front of the firebox. Then, with the craft-knife, remove the Belpaire firebox. Also using the craft knife, remove the steps on the left-hand side of the bunker. With a hacksaw remove the rear of the bunker, then the rear of the cab (**Figure 2**).

Next remove the boiler support from between the two tanks (**Figure 3**), then remove 4mm from the running-plate in the area formerly occupied by the splashers (again **Figure 3**). Then glue together the two parts of the running plate, reinforce the join with a piece of card 30mm x 10mm on the underside, and a piece of paper 34mm x 22mm on the upper side. Next re-assemble the bunker and cab, extending the loco's length by 24mm in the process (**Figure 4**).

Using card or Plasticard manufacture a new rear and front for the cab (**Figure 5**). Also using card or Plasticard, manufacture a new top for the coal-space, 30mm x 24mm, glue in place, paint black and cover with imitation coal. Then manufacture a coal-rail for the top of the bunker from 1mm-diameter wire, 84mm long, bend to shape and glue in place around the top of the bunker.

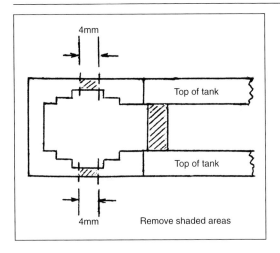

Figure 3: Modifications to front of '1400' body

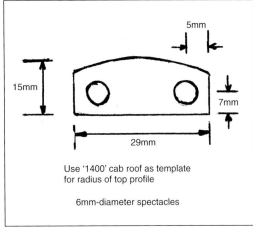

Figure 5: New rear and front for cab

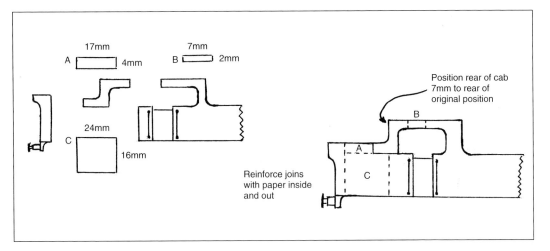

Figure 4: Re-assembly of cab and bunker

Make a new cab roof from card, 32mm x 34mm, bend to shape and glue in place. Then manufacture a cab roof shutter from card – 5mm square – and glue it in place astride the centre-line 4mm from the front edge of the roof. Then manufacture the cab rain-strips from 0.5mm-diameter wire, 25mm long; bend to shape and glue in place.

We now turn our attention to the boiler and smokebox. Having shortened the front of the body by 4mm, we have to modify the boiler accordingly, while at the same time raising the level of the boiler (that of the 'F4' was pitched higher than on the '1400'). First remove the four fixing lugs from the rear of the boiler and the smokebox saddle. Then remove 4mm from the

underside of the boiler (Figure 6). Increase the height of the boiler by adding 2mm-square microstrip to the base of the smokebox saddle and the undersides of the boiler (again Figure 6).

Then drill a 1mm-diameter hole on each side of the boiler, 3mm below the handrails and 10mm to the rear of the smokebox to take the clack-valves. At this point it would be a good idea to drill three 1mm holes through the running-plate above the front buffer-beam, and another through the top of the smokebox 2mm from the front on the centre-line to take the lamp-brackets – I use the Westward variety on all of my models.

Next offer the boiler to the rest of the body and check for a straight and square fit. If

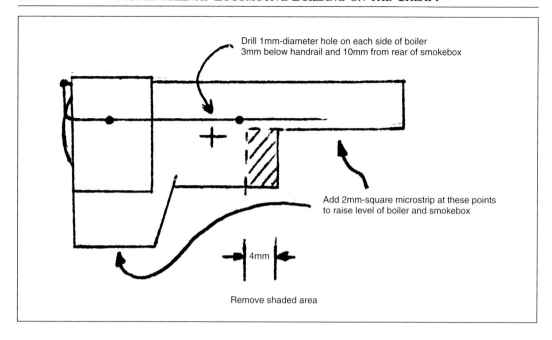

Drill 1mm-diameter hole on each side of boiler
3mm below handrail and 10mm from rear of smokebox

Add 2mm-square microstrip at these points
to raise level of boiler and smokebox

4mm

Remove shaded area

Figure 6: Modifications to boiler and smokebox saddle

satisfactory, glue it in place. Next manufacture a new top for the firebox from a piece of card 19mm wide and 16mm in length; bend it to match the curve of the boiler and glue in place. Cover the top of the firebox with a piece of paper to hide the 'threepenny-bit' effect, then camouflage the joins between the boiler and the tops of the tanks with Milliput, or a piece of paper. Drill a 1mm-diameter hole 3mm from the front of the cab, and 5mm to the right of the centre-line, to take the whistle. Then drill two 1mm-diameter holes, for the safety-valves, on the centre-line, 19mm and 23mm from the front of the cab.

Now we turn to the fitting of the front springs. As these have to be in line with the front axle, it is best done with the body sitting on the chassis. Glue them to the side of the smokebox saddle, in line with the front wheels (I used MJT wagon springs – they look quite good).

Next glue the chimney in place (I used a Dave Alexander Worsdell chimney, from his 'J21' kit) – it goes in the same position as its GWR predecessor. Then glue the dome in place, astride the second boiler-band (again I used the Dave Alexander version from the 'J21' kit). Now paint the boiler black, and, when dry, add the boiler-bands (I used Modelmaster waterslide transfers –

they allow plenty of time for you to slide them around). The rear boiler-band should be 13mm from the cab front, while the third should be 13mm to the rear of the second band. Now varnish the boiler (I used Humbrol 'Satin-Cote' – and very good it is too!), and, when dry, glue the whistle, safety-valves and clack-valves in position.

Glue the Westinghouse pump in position on the right-hand side of the loco. Use photographs as a guide – some locos carried them on the front of the tank, while the majority had them fitted to the boiler side, in-line with the first boiler-band. Next, from a 56mm length of 1mm-diameter wire, manufacture a regulator/vacuum ejector pipe, bend it to shape (use photographs as a guide) and butt-join it to the existing GWR pipe on the side of the smokebox (**Figure 7**). Finally paint the pipe black.

When we extended the bunker we created a gap in the running-plate and the pipe that runs along its underside – fill these gaps with lengths of 1mm wire and paint them black. If you decided not to attach the rear coupling to the loco chassis, you could use a piece of 1mm-diameter wire wrapped around each bufferstock, or you could drill two 1mm-diameter holes through the buffer-beam 7mm either side of the

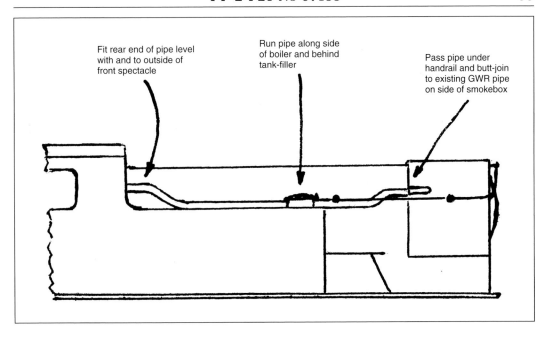

Fit rear end of pipe level with and to outside of front spectacle

Run pipe along side of boiler and behind tank-filler

Pass pipe under handrail and butt-join to existing GWR pipe on side of smokebox

Figure 7: Fitting vacuum ejector pipe

coupling-hook, and use them as the basis for a coupling (with the 1mm-diameter wire again).

Next put a spot of glue on the thread of the pony-truck securing bolt just above the nut – this will prevent it working loose while in traffic.

You can now start the lining and numbering. Be careful when selecting an identity for your model, and work from a photograph if possible.

Some members of the class received lipped Worsdell chimneys (as per my model), while others ran with stovepipe chimneys right through to withdrawal. While most of the locos had their condensing gear removed, some retained this equipment to the end. Some were fitted with 'push and pull' equipment, and dual-braked locos had *two* brake-pipes on each buffer-beam.

# Ex-LNER 'G5' 0-4-4T
# No 67281

In 1894 the North Eastern Railway introduced its Class 'O' 0-4-4 tank locomotives. They were designed by Wilson Worsdell, and when construction ceased in 1901 110 examples had been built. Five locos built in 1896 were fitted experimentally with 'Younghusband's valve-gear' (who?), but after three years this was replaced with Stephenson 'link motion' as fitted to the rest of the class. Originally all the locos had Ramsbottom safety-valves with standard North Eastern brass covers, but under the LNER these were replaced by Ross 'pop' safety-valves, and all of the class had been so treated by the time of nationalisation. All the locos had Westinghouse pumps from new (fitted to the front of the left-hand tank), and from 1914 onwards all were fitted with vacuum brakes (entailing the fitting of an ejector pipe on the right-hand side of the boiler).

In March 1938 LNER No 387 (BR No 67340) was fitted with extended side tanks (somewhat similar in appearance to those of the Southern Railway's 'E2' Class), and retained them until withdrawal in 1958 (when the tanks were extended the Westinghouse pump was removed). In 1937 LNER No 1883 (67281) was fitted for 'push and pull' operation, and between 1937 and 1949 a further 20 were so fitted (including No 387, the loco with extended tanks). All of these locos had their Westinghouse pumps removed.

After the Grouping the locos became LNER Class 'G5', and a small number were tried on other parts of the LNER system – three (all 'push and pull'-fitted) were transferred to Stratford and rotated with ex-Great Eastern locos on the Epping-Ongar and Seven Sisters-Palace Gates services. In 1951 these three locos were transferred to Cambridge for working the Audley End to Bartlow branch, and all three were withdrawn in 1956. Likewise three locos (not 'push and pull'-fitted) were transferred to Scotland and saw service at Parkhead and Dunfermline before moving on to the GNofS section, being allocated to Kittybrewster and Keith. The last of the three (No 67327) was withdrawn in 1955. The class was eventually rendered extinct with the mass withdrawal of 11 North Eastern locos in December 1958.

So we have another large class (110 examples) and a long-lived one (64 years). Moreover, all 110 locos survived to become BR property on 1 January 1948. Examples could be seen in Scotland, East London, East Anglia and, of course, ex-North Eastern territory. Another class worthy of modelling!

## Items required

Dapol '1400' 0-4-2 tank (it is possible to convert the Hornby version, but more work is involved – the rear of the chassis is occupied by a large weight that would have to be removed!); Hornby LNER 'Pacific' power unit pony-truck (L.5136); one pair of 14mm diameter bogie-wheels; detailing parts as described in the text.

## Stage 1: The chassis

After separating the body and chassis, remove the clip-fit rear coupling, then, with a hacksaw or craft-knife, remove the dummy outside frames of the rear axle. Close examination of the rear of the chassis will reveal that it is composed of three layers: at the bottom, the plastic underframe; in the middle, the metal chassis block (note that the plastic underframe wraps around the sides of this block); then finally the

*Above* 'G5' 0-4-4T No 67325 on Malton shed in North Yorkshire on 11 June 1956. *Frank Hornby*

*Below* The completed model.

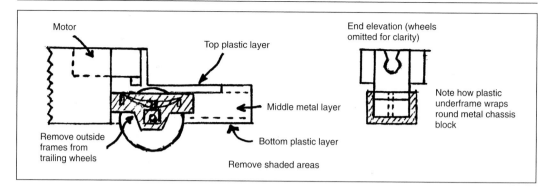

Figure 1: Rear of '1400' chassis

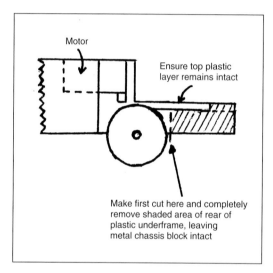

Figure 2: Removal of rear portion of plastic underframe

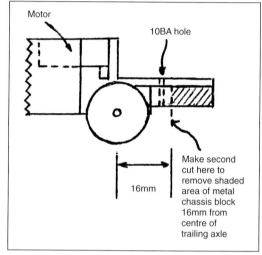

Figure 3: Removal of rear portion of metal chassis block

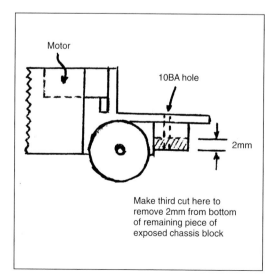

Figure 4: Removal of bottom portion of chassis block

top layer of plastic, including the motor-mount (**Figure 1**). Note also that there is a 10BA hole approximately 14mm to the rear of the motor (this hole is a vital ingredient in this conversion and we will come back to it later).

Now, with a hacksaw or craft-knife remove the rear of the plastic underframe by cutting through the plastic immediately to the rear of the trailing wheels to leave the metal chassis block exposed. *Ensure that you leave the top layer of plastic intact* (**Figure 2**). Again using the hacksaw, cut through the metal chassis block 16mm to the rear of the trailing axle (again *do not damage the top layer of plastic*) (**Figure 3**).

Now make a horizontal cut 2mm from the bottom of the remaining exposed portion of the chassis block (**Figure 4**). Clean the sawn edges with a file, and upon close examination you will

The completed chassis – note the 10BA nut and bolt.

find that the previously mentioned 10BA hole passes through the metal chassis block. This hole will be the pivot-hole for the pony-truck.

We now turn our attention to the pony-truck. At the time of writing the one from the Hornby LNER 'Pacific' power unit (part ref L.5136) is still available as a separate item from both Modelspares and East Kent Models. The only work required on this item is to exchange the Hornby disc wheels for a pair of spoked 14mm-diameter bogie wheels. At this point it is a good idea to add a small weight to the pony-truck to prevent it from bouncing around and derailing. I used a piece of scrap white-metal 9mm x 8mm x 3mm glued to the top of the pony-truck between the wheels. When the glue has dried, take a 16mm-long 10BA nut and bolt and attach the pony-truck to the chassis via the 10BA hole already mentioned – you may need to add some spacing washers to get the pony-truck (and its integral coupling) level. Once this is done you can begin road-testing, and when you are happy with its performance add some glue to the 10BA nut and bolt to prevent them from working loose. Your chassis is now complete, and furthermore you have created a previously unknown wheel arrangement – 0-4-2-2!

## Stage 2: the body

First of all separate the boiler and smokebox from the rest of the body. This moulding is held in place by four lugs, two under the firebox and two under the base of the smokebox saddle. At this point remove all four lugs with a craft-knife and file flush the underside of the smokebox saddle. When the body and chassis were separated, the GWR-style chimney will have come away at the same time, but we still need to file the remains of its base flush with the top of the smokebox. Then, with the craft-knife,

remove the top-feed and its associated pipework, together with the strange GWR pipe on the top of the smokebox just behind the chimney. As regards the other GWR pipe on the side of the smokebox (just above the handrail), this can be used as part of the vacuum ejector pipe, so just cut away the part of the pipe that overlaps onto the boiler. Next remove the dome and file its remains flush with the boiler, then fill the hole with Milliput or similar and, when set, file flush with the boiler.

Unfortunately for us, the 'G5s' did not have continuous handrails, so we will have to remove the front part that curves around the top of the smokebox door. With a hacksaw or wire-cutters, snip through the handrails approximately 5mm from the front of the smokebox, and remove the front portion of the handrail. Next we need to raise the level of the smokebox in relation to the running-plate (the 'G5s' had higher-pitched boilers than the '1400s'), so cut out two pieces of 1mm-thick Plasticard 7mm x 4mm and glue them, one on top of the other, to the front of the underside of the smokebox saddle, thus increasing the height by 2mm.

Next cut out a piece of 1mm-thick Plasticard 40mm x 16mm and glue it to the underside of the rear portion of the boiler (the part that sits on top of the tanks). Now cut out a piece of card 15mm x 25mm to form the top of the firebox, bend it to shape and glue it in place at the rear end of the boiler. When the glue has dried, cut out a piece of paper 40mm x 32mm and glue that in place, wrapped around the rear portion of the boiler, including the firebox – this will hide the joins and 'threepenny-bit' effect. When the glue has dried, drill three 1mm-diameter holes through the top of the firebox on the centre-line at 4mm intervals from the cab front (for the whistle and safety-valves).

We now turn our attention to the rest of the

body. First, with the craft-knife, remove the Belpaire firebox, the 'mushroom' vents, the water-fillers, and the rest of the moulded detail from the tops of the tanks (take care when removing the water-fillers – we'll be using them again!). Next, with a penknife blade, remove the small handrail from the rear left-hand side of the cab roof, then remove the roof and rear of the cab (these are both the same moulding and are only glued in place) – again, take care not to damage this part as we shall be re-using part of it! Then remove the coal moulding from the top of the bunker (again only glued in place). Using the craft-knife, remove the splasher tool-boxes, and, with the penknife blade, remove the tank fronts (one complete moulding – only glued in place).

Again using the craft-knife, remove the raised edge from the top of each tank and file flush. Then cut out two pieces of 1mm-thick Plasticard 39mm x 13mm and glue them, one on top of the other, to the tops of the tanks (thus raising the level of the tanks by 2mm). Then cut out two pieces of Plasticard 17mm x 10mm to form the new tank fronts, and glue them in place. Now manufacture the new tank sides from paper **(Figure 5)** and glue them in place with PVA adhesive, ensuring that the top edge of the paper is in line with the newly fitted tank tops and that the leading edges of the paper are wrapped around the front of each tank. Also ensure that the rear edges of the paper are lined up with the cab cut-out.

While the PVA is drying, cut out two pieces of paper 14mm x 4mm and glue them over the holes in the running-plate caused by the removal

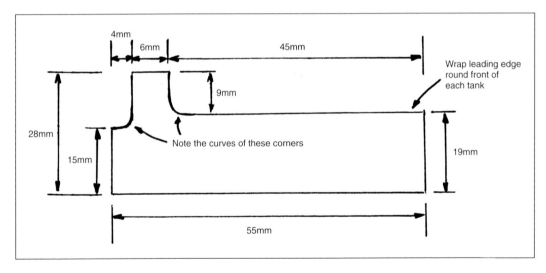

*Above* **Figure 5: New tank sides**

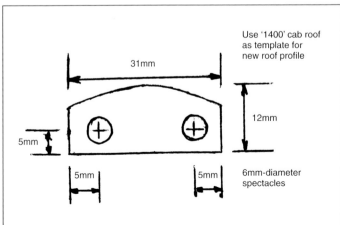

*Left* **Figure 6: New cab front**

of the splasher tool-boxes. When the glue of the tank extension work has set (hopefully rock-hard!) we can remove the cab front of the '1400', then manufacture a replacement from Plasticard (**Figure 6**), and glue in place.

Now we move on to the dissection of the cab and bunker. With a hacksaw or craft-knife, make three cuts on each side of the loco as in **Figure 7**. At the same time remove the two steps from the left-hand side of the bunker, taking care not to damage the cab handrails, then clean up the edges of the saw-cuts.

Next manufacture a floor for the cab and bunker from Plasticard or wood 31mm x 29mm (**Figure 8**). Drill a 4mm-diameter hole on the centre-line, 6mm from one end. Then, with the body sitting on the chassis, glue the new cab/bunker in position with the 4mm hole over the 10BA nut and bolt.

When the glue has dried, re-assemble the cab and bunker (**Figure 9**), manufacturing the new parts from 1mm-thick Plasticard. Following re-assembly, cover the sides of the bunker with paper to hide and reinforce the joins. As regards the gaps in the top of each cab-side, wrap and glue a piece of paper around them using PVA adhesive.

Next take the '1400' cab roof moulding and remove the rear with a craft-knife, then glue it in place at the rear of the new cab. Make a new cab roof from card 35mm x 28mm, bend it to shape and glue in place.

Now we turn our attention to the top of the bunker. Most of the 'G5s' (generally the ones that remained on the North Eastern) had 'cage' bunkers, whereas those that emigrated to Scotland and the Great Eastern had their cages removed (use photographs as a guide). If you decide to model one of the 'cage'-bunker variety (these were the most numerous, after all), you could fashion the cage from lengths of wire soldered together; while this would look very authentic, it would involve a lot of hard work. I built my 'cage' from card covered with Slater's Plasticard 'corrugated iron' (sheet No 0436) (**Figure 10**).

Paint the bunker black and add the coal – I re-used the coal moulding from the '1400' cut down to fit inside the 'cage'.

Next, using card or Plasticard, manufacture the cab-roof ventilator – 5mm square – and glue in place 23mm from the front of the cab, astride the centre-line. Then make the rain-strips for the roof from 23mm lengths of handrail wire,

Figure 7: Cuts to cab and bunker

Figure 8: New cab/bunker floor

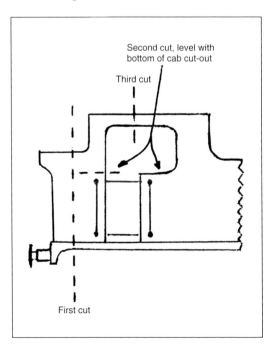

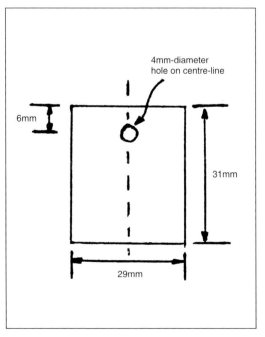

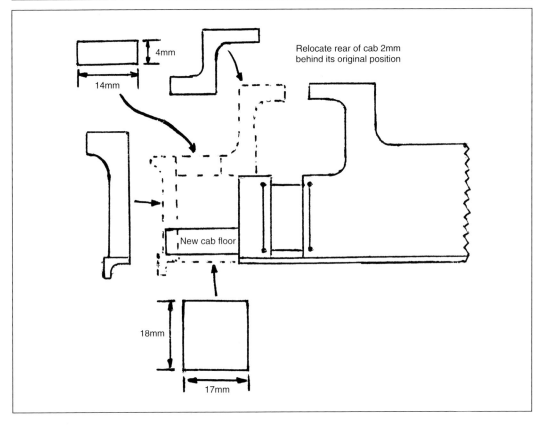

4mm

14mm

Relocate rear of cab 2mm
behind its original position

New cab floor

18mm

17mm

*Above* Figure 9: Re-assembly of bunker and cab

*Below* Figure 10: Construction of 'cage' bunker

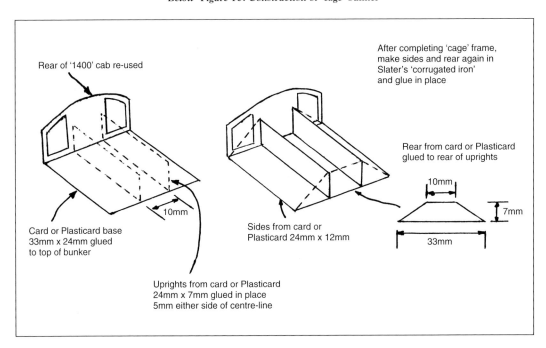

Rear of '1400' cab re-used

After completing 'cage' frame,
make sides and rear again in
Slater's 'corrugated iron'
and glue in place

Rear from card or Plasticard
glued to rear of uprights

10mm

7mm

10mm

33mm

Card or Plasticard base
33mm x 24mm glued
to top of bunker

Sides from card or
Plasticard 24mm x 12mm

Uprights from card or Plasticard
24mm x 7mm glued in place
5mm either side of centre-line

bent to shape and glued in place (again use photographs as a guide).

We now turn our attention to the front of the loco. If, like me, you are using Westward lamp-brackets, drill three 1mm-diameter holes in the usual positions through the running-plate immediately above the buffer-beam. Comparing photographs of 'G5s' and '1400s', the former had much greater front overhangs than the latter. It is possible to increase the front overhang of the model by 4mm without the need to modify the front couplings. First, with a hacksaw, cut through the running-plate 7mm to the rear of the front buffer-beam. Then cut out a piece of Plasticard 4mm x 33mm, together with two pieces 4mm x 2mm, and re-assemble the front end as **Figure 11**.

Next we turn our attention to the boiler and smokebox. First fit the curved handrail to the top of the smokebox (use photographs as a guide). Next drill a 1mm-diameter hole through the top of the smokebox, on the centre-line, in front of the chimney to take the top lamp-bracket. Fit a Worsdell chimney in the same position as its GWR predecessor, then fit a Worsdell dome. The position of the dome varied according to the type of boiler fitted, but the majority of 'G5s' had the centre of their domes in line with the ends of the tanks (again use photographs as a guide). The chimney and dome on my model are from the Dave Alexander range (from his 'J21' kit). Fit the whistle and Ross 'pop' safety-valves into the holes that you have already drilled in the top of the firebox; the safety-valves on my model

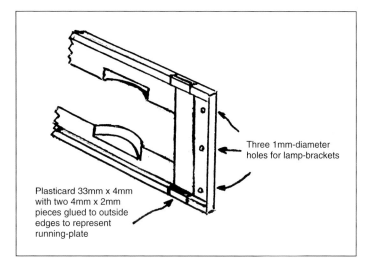

**Figure 11: Increasing front overhang (buffer-beam omitted for clarity)**

Three 1mm-diameter holes for lamp-brackets

Plasticard 33mm x 4mm with two 4mm x 2mm pieces glued to outside edges to represent running-plate

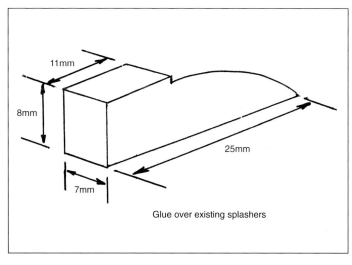

11mm

8mm

7mm

25mm

Glue over existing splashers

**Figure 12: Combined splashers and sand-boxes for front wheels**

come from the Hornby 'D49' (supplied by East Kent Models).

Now glue the boiler to the body and fit the tank water-fillers (I re-used the original ex-GWR '1400' examples, which have a vague resemblance to the North Eastern pattern). Using card or Plasticard manufacture the combined front splashers and sandboxes as in **Figure 12**, and glue them in place over the existing splashers.

Make a vacuum ejector pipe from 1mm-diameter wire, bend to shape (use photographs as a guide) and glue in place on the right-hand side of the loco, running from the cab to link up with the ex-GWR pipe on the side of the smokebox. Then use the same size of wire to plug the gaps in the vacuum brake pipes (they run along the underside of the running-plate on each side) at the points where we lengthened the locomotive. Then use the 1mm-diameter wire again to plug the gaps in the running-plate where we lengthened the bunker. Next manufacture a 'piano-front' from a 13mm

length of 2mm-square microstrip or balsa, or even (dare I say it?) a matchstick! File it to a quadrant shape (use photographs as a guide) and glue it in place at the front of the smokebox saddle.

Now, depending on the identity of your chosen model, fit a Westinghouse pump to the front of the left-hand tank (castings are available from many manufacturers) or fit 'push and pull' equipment to the right-hand side of the smokebox (castings for this equipment are available from Autocomm Ltd (formerly Nu-Cast) and Alan Gibson). For the 'push and pull' variant you will need *two* brake-pipes on each buffer-beam.

Finally, 13 locos had their Westinghouse brake equipment removed after nationalisation, thus carrying neither a Westinghouse pump nor 'push and pull' equipment). These locos were Nos 67243/47/51/60/63/64/70/98/300/04/07/10/48, and of course they only had *one* brake-pipe on each buffer-beam. In BR days the 'G5s' were painted black with mixed-traffic lining.

# Ex-LNER 'L1' 2-6-4T No 67723

During the 1930s the LNER's 'top-link' suburban passenger loco was Gresley's 'V1' Class of 2-6-2 tanks, introduced to service in 1930. However, by the end of the decade it had become clear that something more powerful would be needed, as by that time trains were getting heavier and passengers were pressing for faster journey times. A number of 'V1s' were modified to run at a higher boiler pressure (Class 'V3', introduced in 1939), but this remedy was only short-lived and the problem was back again by 1942/3. Edward Thompson's solution was to stretch the 'V3' into a 2-6-4, and this became his 'L1' Class, introduced to service in 1945. When construction ceased in 1950 a total of 100 locos had been built, and they could be seen on almost all parts of the LNER. In their early years a number worked on the Glasgow suburban lines, but these had all been transferred to England by the mid-1950s. The NE Region had a large allocation serving the large conurbations of Middlesbrough, Hull and the West Riding, while the Eastern Region had allocations at Doncaster, Grantham, Colwick, Cambridge, Norwich, Ipswich, Stratford and King's Cross. They could also be seen on the Great Central section from Marylebone in the south to Manchester and Liverpool in the north.

They were enigmatic engines – opinions varied, from a Cambridge driver I knew who always referred to them as 'Cement-mixers' (apparently riding in the cab was like riding in a cement-mixer!) to an Ipswich man who thought they were greatest thing since sliced bread! (They must have been some good or they wouldn't have built 100 of them!) Electrification and dieselisation of suburban services meant the end for them and the last example (No 67800) was withdrawn from Langwith Junction (41J) in December 1962, after a career of only 12 years! If you have an LNER layout set in the BR period an 'L1' would be a useful addition.

As far as modelling specific examples is concerned, all locos up to No 67739 inclusive had Westinghouse brakes fitted (as well as vacuum), so a Westinghouse pump was fitted to the right-hand side of the smokebox, together with *two* brake-pipes on each buffer-beam. All locos up to No 67730 inclusive had a quadrant between the running-plate and the buffer-beam, while all the others had a gap between the two, allowing access to the fronts of the valve-chests. All locos had electric headlamps powered by a Stones generator on the right-hand running-plate beside the smokebox.

## Items required

Bachmann 'V3' 2-6-2T (preferably with straight steam-pipes and original bunker); two pairs of Jackson 12mm-diameter bogie-wheels; detailing parts as described in the text.

## Stage 1: The chassis

First remove the rear pony-truck from the chassis. Having done this you will notice that it was kept in contact with the track by a spring on a plastic pillar. We will use this pillar to attach the new four-wheel bogie, but in order to enable the bogie to swing, remove the rear corners of the plastic underframe adjacent to the pillar (**Figure 1**).

Next manufacture a new rear bogie from 'Plastruct' rectangular tubing 9.5mm x 6.4mm (**Figure 2**). Note that the pivot-hole for the swing-link has to be countersunk on the bottom of the bogie. Note also that the top front corners

*Above* 'L1' 2-6-4 No 67716 at Darlington on 10 June 1956. *John Edgington*

*Below* The completed model.

*Right*  Figure 1: Modification to underside of rear of 'V3' chassis

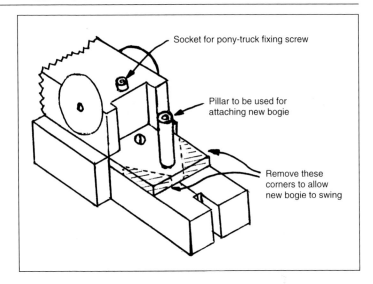

Socket for pony-truck fixing screw

Pillar to be used for attaching new bogie

Remove these corners to allow new bogie to swing

*Below*  Figure 2: New rear bogie

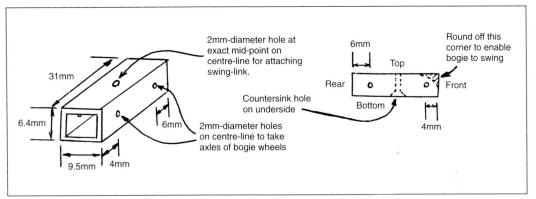

31mm

6.4mm

9.5mm    4mm

6mm

2mm-diameter hole at exact mid-point on centre-line for attaching swing-link.

Countersink hole on underside

2mm-diameter holes on centre-line to take axles of bogie wheels

6mm

Rear    Top    Bottom    Front

4mm

Round off this corner to enable bogie to swing

need to be filed away to enable the bogie to swing around the pillar.

Next glue a Dapol plastic coupling to the inside top edge of the rear end of the bogie, then cover the remaining gap with a piece of card or Plasticard 9mm x 4mm (**Figure 3**).

Manufacture the swing-link from Plasticard or thin brass as in **Figure 4**, ensuring that the large hole fits over the pillar and rotates freely. Then attach the swing-link to the bogie using a 10mm-long *countersunk* 10BA nut and bolt, together with a brass washer between the link and the bogie. Then fit the wheels and check that they run freely, adding a small piece of scrap white-metal to the rear of the bogie (between the wheels) to add a bit of stability to the ensemble. Fit the swing-link over the pillar, check that the bogie swings freely, and, if so, replace the original

Glue Dapol plastic (Delrin) coupling to inside top edge of rear of bogie

Cover remaining gap with card or Plasticard 9mm x 4mm

*Right*  Figure 3: Fitting rear coupling

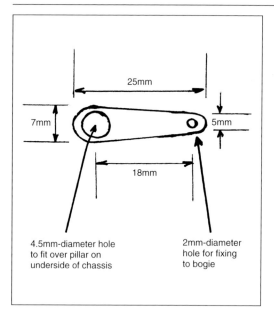

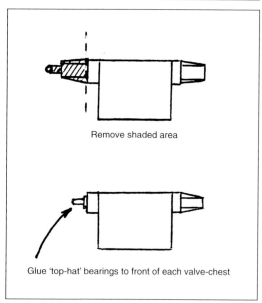

Figure 4:  Dimensions of swing-link

Figure 5: Modifications to cylinders

self-tapping screw from the Bachmann 'V3' to hold the swing-link (and the chassis) in place. Now paint the bogie-frame black.

Finally, use a craft-knife to remove the extensions of the cylinder valve spindles (part of the famous Gresley 'derived motion') from the front of each valve-chest, and file away any residue. Then glue a 'top-hat' bearing to the front of each valve-chest (Figure 5). Your chassis is now ready for road-testing.

## Stage 2: The body

First remove the 'V3' dome with a hacksaw, fill in the resulting hole with Milliput or similar, and, when the filler has set, file the residue flush with the boiler. Next remove the handrails from the rear of the bunker and the tops of the tanks, then remove the rear 15mm of the boiler handrails. Using a craft-knife, remove the splashers, then, if using a loco with 'elbowed' steam-pipes, cut or file these down to a straight profile (use photographs as a guide). Remove the coal insert from the top of the bunker, together with the rear of the cab (both parts of the same moulding), and, if using one of the locos with an original bunker, separate the coal insert and retain for further use.

Next remove the bunker with a vertical

hacksaw cut immediately behind the cab, then remove the top 6mm of the bunker (**Figure 6**). Using a craft-knife, remove the remains of the upper footstep from the bunker side.

Next re-assemble the lower portion of the bunker (**Figure 7**). First cut out two pieces of 1mm-thick Plasticard 10mm x 22mm and glue them to the sides of the rear of the bunker. Glue this new assembly to the rear of the cab, while at the same time reinforcing the joins with a piece of paper 133mm x 15mm glued around the inside of the bunker and cab with PVA adhesive (which soaks into the paper and sets rock-hard!). Next, from Plasticard, wood or balsa, manufacture a bunker floor 29mm x 13mm and glue it inside the rear of the bunker (to add stability) approximately 10mm below the top edge. The enlargement of the bunker has created a 10mm gap in the running-plate on each side of the loco, which can be plugged with lengths of 1mm-diameter wire glued in place. Next cover the outside panels of the bunker with pieces of paper 36mm x 22mm to hide the joins (ever heard the expression 'papering over the cracks'…?).

Cut out a piece of card or Plasticard 30mm x 34mm and glue it over the top of the bunker – note that this should overhang the rear of the bunker by approximately 1mm. Then

*Right* **Figure 6:** Removal of bunker

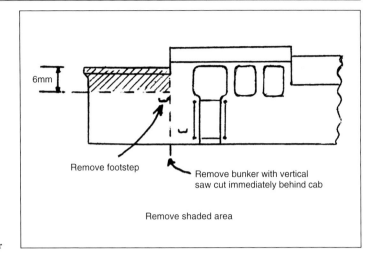

6mm

Remove footstep

Remove bunker with vertical
saw cut immediately behind cab

Remove shaded area

*Below* **Figure 7:** Re-assembly of bunker

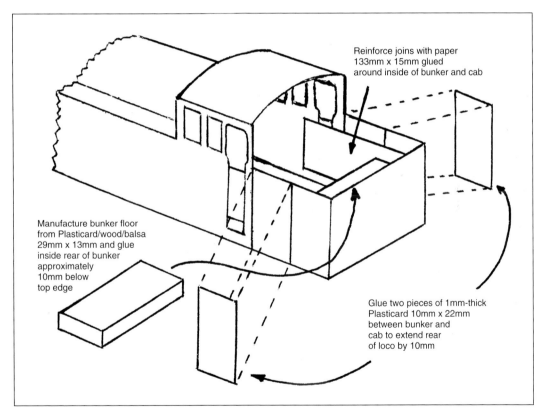

Reinforce joins with paper
133mm x 15mm glued
around inside of bunker and cab

Manufacture bunker floor
from Plasticard/wood/balsa
29mm x 13mm and glue
inside rear of bunker
approximately
10mm below
top edge

Glue two pieces of 1mm-thick
Plasticard 10mm x 22mm
between bunker and
cab to extend rear
of loco by 10mm

manufacture the coal space from card or Plasticard (**Figure 8**), and re-use the original coal-insert from the 'V3'.

Now we come to the extensions of the side tanks. Take two pieces of card or Plasticard 5mm x 14mm and glue them to the running-plate (in an upright position) on each side of the locomotive 7mm to the rear of the leading boiler-band. Then, from card or Plasticard, manufacture the extension side (**Figure 9**), and glue in place.

Cut out two pieces of thin card 5mm x 25mm to form the tops of the tank extensions, and glue them in place. Next cut out two pieces of paper (**Figure 10**) and glue them over the tank extensions to hide the joins.

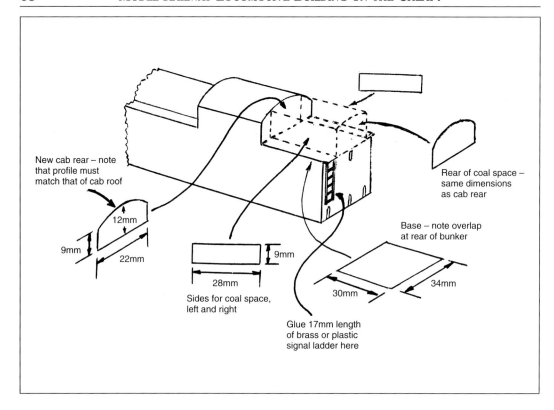

New cab rear – note
that profile must
match that of cab roof

Rear of coal space –
same dimensions
as cab rear

Base – note overlap
at rear of bunker

12mm

9mm

22mm

9mm

28mm

34mm

30mm

Sides for coal space,
left and right

Glue 17mm length
of brass or plastic
signal ladder here

*Above* Figure 8: New coal space

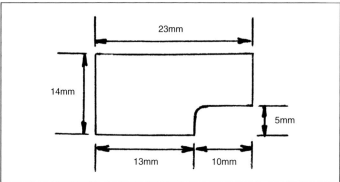

23mm

14mm

5mm

13mm

10mm

*Left* Figure 9: Dimensions of side
tank extensions

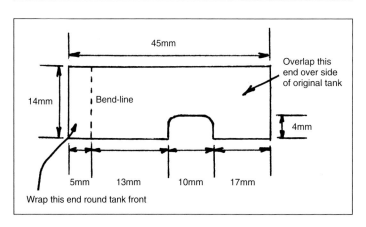

45mm

Overlap this
end over side
of original tank

14mm

Bend-line

4mm

5mm      13mm      10mm      17mm

Wrap this end round tank front

*Left* Figure 10: Dimensions of paper
covers for side tanks

Fit a Westinghouse pump to the front of the right-hand tank (these are available from a large number of manufacturers including Alan Gibson, South-Eastern Finecast, and Dave Alexander). Then fit the new dome. The 'L1s' had standard domes as fitted to the 'B17s', 'D49s', 'K1s', etc, and these are available from Dave Alexander, Markits and one or two others – on my model I used the Markits 'D49' version. The dome is fitted 2mm ahead of the third boiler-band (in line with the maintenance hole in the side of each tank).

Next fit a Wakefield lubricator to the running-plate on each side of the loco, just in front of the leading boiler-band. These are available from Dave Alexander, Craftsman Models, Markits and Alan Gibson, among others. Fit a pair of sand-box fillers immediately in front of the steam-pipes on each side of the loco – the filler on the right-hand side may need filing narrower to accommodate the Stones generator alongside it (use photographs as a guide). White-metal castings for the sand-box fillers are available from Craftsman Models, Dave Alexander and Westward Models, while a casting for the Stones generator is available from Dave Alexander.

Electric headlamps are available from Dave Alexander in a set of six (from his Bulleid and BR Standard tender kits). Fit the top one at the very top of the smokebox door, one in front of each of the outside lamp brackets on the buffer-beam, and *two* in front of the centre lamp-bracket (use photographs as a guide). Then fit two brake-pipes (dual-fitted) to each buffer-beam, one on each side of the coupling. The loco is now ready for painting and transfers: the livery carried during BR days was 'mixed-traffic', and the route availability was 'RA6'.

# Ex-LNER 'J73' 0-6-0T No 68363

The Class 'J73' was designed by Wilson Worsdell, and was the largest of the North Eastern 0-6-0 tank designs. The locomotives were introduced in 1891 and only ten were built. Two of them, LNER Nos 544 and 545 (BR Nos 68355 and 68356) were commandeered for war service in 1914, and spent the next four years propelling armoured trains in Northumberland and North Yorkshire. For these duties they were equipped with Westinghouse brakes with *two* pumps – one at each leading corner of the smokebox – and condensing apparatus (including 'mushroom' vents on the top of each tank). At the end of the war the right-hand pump and the condensing apparatus was removed (but the vents were left in situ). Between 1928 and 1930 these same two locos were fitted with vacuum brakes, which involved the fitting of an ejector pipe along the left-hand side of the boiler, together with two brake-pipes (dual-brakes). Between 1944 and 1946 both the Westinghouse and vacuum-braking equipment was removed (but the 'mushroom' vents remained).

All ten members of the class survived to become BR property in 1948. In 1950 four of them were allocated to West Hartlepool and three to Selby, while the remaining three were allocated to Springhead. Unfortunately, by the end of 1958 the onset of the diesel-shunter combined with a lack of traffic had brought their number down to five. The West Hartlepool allocation was down to two, while Selby shed had closed and its three 'J73s' had gone for scrap. Springhead had closed to steam and two of its 'J73s' (Nos 68360 and 68361) had moved to Dairycoates, while the third (No 68363) had moved to Botanic to become shed pilot there. Sadly, Botanic closed to steam on 1 June 1959

and No 68363 moved across to Dairycoates, it was withdrawn in October 1959. The class became extinct in 1960 when No 68361 was withdrawn from Dairycoates in November of that year

The 'J73s' were not a very large class, and were not very widespread, but they were certainly long-lived (69 years!). A model of one would certainly be something different!

## Items required

Hornby 'Jinty' 0-6-0T; detailing parts as described in the text.

## Making the model

First of all separate the body from the chassis – they are held together by three lugs, two under the smokebox saddle and one in the rear of the bunker. Thankfully there are no modifications required to the chassis!

Remove the Midland-type regulator pipe from the right-hand side of the loco (it fits over the boiler handrail). Next remove the chimney and dome, and file flush any residue.

We now move to the smokebox door. Some modellers may prefer to drill out the existing LMS-pattern door altogether and fit a new one, and suitable castings are produced by Dave Alexander (from his 'J21' kit) and Autocomm Ltd (from their Nu-Cast 'N8' kit). However, it is possible to modify the existing 'Jinty' door. First remove the handrail above the numberplate with a penknife blade, then, using a craft-knife, carefully remove the six 'dog clips' from the door's outer rim. Next, if you are planning to use a Markits smokebox door handle, drill a 1mm-diameter hole through the exact centre of the

*Above* One of Selby's three 'J73s', No 68357, on shed on 29 September 1956. *David Holmes*

*Below* The completed model of 'J73' No 68363. The bike on the running-plate was a trademark of the Hull district (if you didn't want to lose it, you kept it with you at all times!).

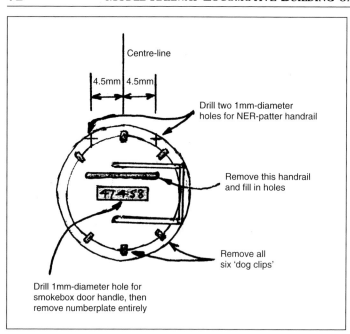

Centre-line

4.5mm | 4.5mm

Drill two 1mm-diameter
holes for NER-patter handrail

Remove this handrail
and fill in holes

Remove all
six 'dog clips'

Drill 1mm-diameter hole for
smokebox door handle, then
remove numberplate entirely

Figure 1: Modifications to smokebox
door

*Below* Figure 2: Construction of
new cab sides

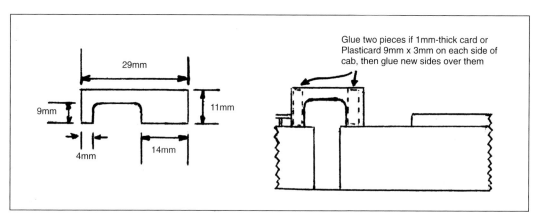

29mm

9mm

11mm

4mm

14mm

Glue two pieces if 1mm-thick card or
Plasticard 9mm x 3mm on each side of
cab, then glue new sides over them

*Below* Figure 3: New cab rear

*Below* Figure 4: New cab front

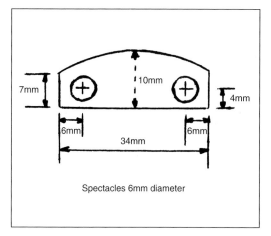

7mm

10mm

6mm

34mm

6mm

4mm

Spectacles 6mm diameter

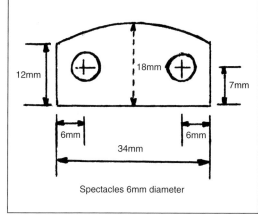

12mm

18mm

7mm

6mm

34mm

6mm

Spectacles 6mm diameter

door. You will find this task easier if you leave the LMS-style numberplate in situ (the centre-point of the numberplate is also the centre-point of the door). Once you've drilled the hole you can remove the numberplate with a craft-knife.

While you are working with the drill on the front end of the loco, also drill three 1mm-diameter holes through the running-plate, just above the front buffer-beam, to take the lamp-brackets (one above the coupling and the others 2mm in from the outside edges of the running-plate). The loco will also need a couple of 1mm-diameter holes in the top of the smokebox front, 4.5mm on either side of the centre-line, to take an NER-pattern handrail (**Figure 1**). Using Milliput or similar, fill the two holes in the smokebox door left by the removal of the LMS-pattern handrail.

Using a craft-knife, remove the small ventilators from the top of each tank. Then remove the Belpaire firebox (retaining the whistle and safety-valves for further use). Next file away the lamp-brackets (plastic mouldings) from the rear of the bunker. Then cut out four pieces of 1mm-thick card or Plasticard 9mm x 3mm and glue them to the outside corners of the cab. Next manufacture new cab sides from card or Plasticard (**Figure 2**), and glue then in place – the new cab sides should now be level with the tank and bunker sides.

Also using card or Plasticard, manufacture a new cab rear (**Figure 3**) and a new cab front (**Figure 4**), and glue them in place.

Next manufacture a new cab roof from card, 31mm long by 38mm wide, bend it to shape and glue it in place over the old roof. Also make a new round-top firebox from card, 13mm long by 20mm wide, and again bend it to shape and glue it in place. Then cover the new firebox with paper (to hide the joins and the 'threepenny-bit' effect). When the glue has dried paint the top of the firebox black, and, when the paint has dried, drill three 1mm-diameter holes on the centre-line at 3mm intervals to take the whistle and safety-valves.

Next, from 1mm-thick card or Plasticard, manufacture a new bunker rear, 34mm wide by 13mm high. File the top to fit the curve of the Jinty's bunker (**Figure 5**), then glue in place. Cut out a piece of paper 17mm high by 66mm long and glue it in place, wrapped around the sides and rear of the bunker (again to hide the joins). Next fill in the sand-box fillers (set in the tank sides) with Milliput or similar and, when dry, file flush with emery-cloth.

Then manufacture new tank sides from paper (**Figure 6**), and glue them in place over the tank sides (thus hiding the joins). Using card or Plasticard, manufacture the combined front splashers and sand-boxes (**Figure 7**), and glue them over the old splashers.

Make the cab ventilator from card 6mm

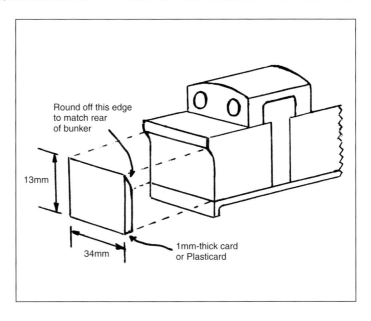

Figure 5: Modification to rear of bunker

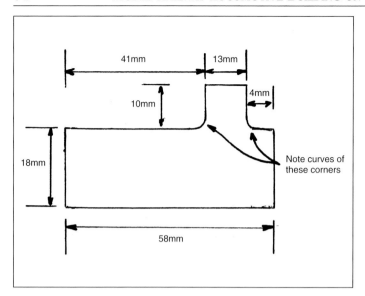

Figure 6: New tank sides

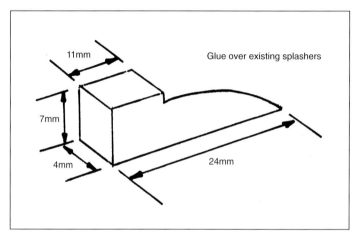

Figure 7: New front splashers

square, bend to shape and glue to the cab roof astride the centre-line 6mm from the leading edge. Next manufacture the rain-strips for the roof from 31mm-long pieces of fine handrail wire, bent to shape and glued in place. Then fit the smokebox dart (I used a Markits one – fiddly, but very good once assembled). Fit the whistle and safety-valves into the three holes that you drilled in the top of the smokebox, re-using the items from the 'Jinty'.

Next glue the front lamp-brackets into the holes that you drilled earlier (I used Westward lamp-brackets, and very good they are too!).

Manufacture the rear lamp-brackets – I used three 3mm lengths of 1mm-square microstrip – and glue them in place on the rear of the bunker. Next glue the dome and chimney in place in the same positions as their LMS predecessors, ensuring that they are square and straight. I used Dave Alexander castings for both items (from his 'J21' kit) – they are very good-quality castings. Finally fit a curved handrail to the front of the smokebox, just above the door (use photographs as a guide).

Your model is now ready for painting. The livery carried was always unlined black, and the route availability was 'RA6'.

# Ex-SR 'O2' 0-4-4T No 30192

In 1889 the London & South Western Railway introduced its 'O2' class of 0-4-4 tanks, designed by William Adams. Sixty locos were originally built, of which 48 still survived at nationalisation, 27 on the mainland and 21 on the Isle of Wight. The locos that saw service on the Isle of Wight were rebuilt with larger bunkers and dual-brakes, ie Westinghouse pumps on the sides of the smokeboxes and circular air reservoir tanks on top of the left-hand water tanks. At the end of 1961 there were still 19 on the Isle of Wight, but only seven remained on the mainland – one at Eastleigh, two at Exmouth Junction, and four at Plymouth (Friary). So here is another long-lived class (70-plus years), and another 'must' for modellers of the 'Withered Arm'.

## Items required

Dapol '1400' 0-4-2 tank (it is possible to convert the Hornby version, but more work is involved – the rear of the chassis is occupied by a large weight that would have to be removed!); Hornby LNER 'Pacific' power unit pony-truck (L.5136); one pair of 14mm diameter bogie-wheels; detailing parts as described in the text.

## Stage 1: The chassis

Many of the processes involved in the early stages of building this model are basically the same as for the LNER 'G5' 0-4-4T (see pages 54-57). After separating the body and chassis, remove the clip-fit rear coupling, then, with a hacksaw or craft-knife, remove the dummy outside frames of the rear axle. Close examination of the rear of the chassis will reveal that it is composed of three layers: at the bottom, the plastic underframe; in the middle, the metal chassis block); finally a top layer of plastic, including the motor-mount (**Figure 1**). Note also that there is a 10BA hole approximately 14mm to the rear of the motor (this hole is a vital ingredient in this conversion and we will come back to it later).

Using a hacksaw or craft-knife remove the rear of the plastic underframe by cutting through the plastic immediately to the rear of the trailing wheels to leave the metal chassis block exposed. *Ensure that you leave the top layer of plastic intact* (**Figure 2**).

Again with the hacksaw, cut through the metal chassis block 16mm to the rear of the trailing axle (again do not damage the top layer of plastic) (**Figure 3**).

Then make a horizontal cut 2mm from the bottom of the remaining exposed portion of chassis block (**Figure 4**). With a file clean up the sawn edges. Upon close examination you will find that the previously mentioned 10BA hole passes through the metal chassis block, and this hole will be the pivot hole for the pony-truck.

Now we turn our attention to the pony-truck from the Hornby LNER 'Pacific' power unit (part ref L.5136), which at the time of writing is still available as a separate item from Modelspares and East Kent Models. The only work required on this item is to exchange the Hornby disc wheels for a pair of spoked 14mm diameter bogie wheels. At this point it is a good idea to add a small weight to the pony-truck to prevent it from bouncing around and derailing. I used a piece of scrap white-metal 9mm x 8mm x 3mm glued to the top of the pony-truck, between the wheels. When the glue has dried, take a 16mm-long 10BA nut and bolt and attach the pony-truck to the chassis via the 10BA hole

*Above* A mainland 'O2' on the 'Withered Arm': No 30200 photographed at Wadebridge on 22 May 1952. *John Edgington*

*Below* The finished model of No 30192. Note the Jackson-Evans etched-brass spectacle surrounds.

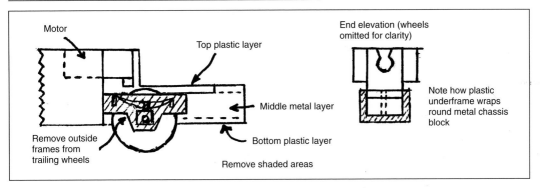

**Figure 1: Rear of '1400' chassis**

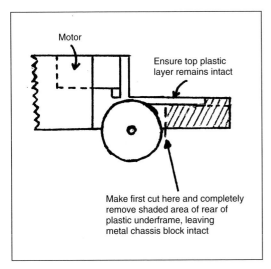

Figure 2: Removal of rear portion of plastic underframe

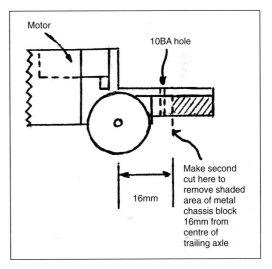

Figure 3: Removal of rear portion of metal chassis block

already mentioned; you may need to add some extra spacing washers to get the pony-truck (and its integral coupling) level. Once this is done you can begin road-testing and, when you are happy with the performance, add some glue to the 10BA nut and bolt to prevent them from working loose. Your chassis is now complete.

## Stage 2: The body

When we separated the body and chassis, the GWR-style chimney will have come away from the body at the same time, but we still need to file the remains of its base flush with the top of the smokebox. Then, with a craft-knife, remove the top-feed and its associated pipework together with the two strange pipes (peculiar to GWR designs) that connect the boiler and smokebox –

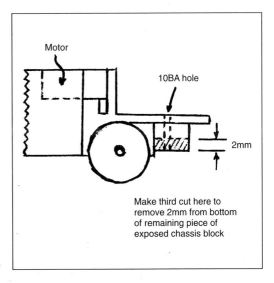

Figure 4: Removal of bottom portion of chassis block

The completed chassis. Note the 10BA nut and bolt.

I believe that they are part of the lubrication system. Once they are gone and filed flush, move on to the dome and file away the 'nipple' from its top; without the 'nipple' its profile is just right for an Adams dome! Next remove the 'mushroom' vents from the tops of the tanks, which are only glued in place.

Now move on to the cab and remove the small handrail from the rear left-hand side of the roof with a penknife blade. Then remove the roof and rear of the cab (both the same moulding and again only glued in place). Remove the coal from the bunker, which again is only glued in place.

Next remove the boiler and smokebox. This moulding is held in place by four lugs, two under the firebox and two under the smokebox saddle. At this point remove the two lugs that fitted underneath the firebox, as they will not be used again. Next, with a pair of small pliers, remove

the GWR whistles from the top of the firebox. With a craft-knife, remove the Belpaire firebox. This is part of the main body moulding, so three cuts are required – two along each side to separate it from the tanks, and a third to separate it from the cab front. Next, with the craft-knife, remove the tool-boxes from the sides of the splashers.

We now come to the dissection of the GWR cab and bunker – carry this out with careful reference to **Figure 5**. With the hacksaw or craft-knife, make your first cut horizontally around the sides and rear of the bunker from doorway to doorway, *ensuring that the cut is level with the tops of the loco tanks*. Then make the second cut, a vertical one approximately halfway along the bunker top, thus removing the top rear portion of the bunker. Then with a third cut remove the curved portion of the rear of the bunker. The

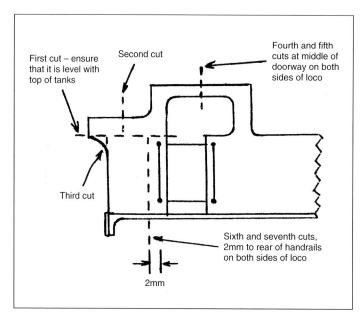

Figure 5: Cuts to cab and bunker

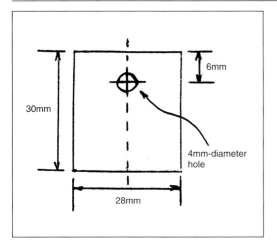

Figure 6: New cab/bunker floor

fourth and fifth cuts are through the top of each doorway at the halfway point, then the sixth and seventh are vertical cuts on each side of the body 2mm to the rear of the rear-most handrails – *take care not to damage the handrails*.

Next manufacture a new cab and bunker floor from a piece of wood or Plasticard 30mm x 28mm, and drill a 4mm-diameter hole 6mm from one end (**Figure 6**). With the body in place on the chassis, apply glue to the front 10mm of each side of the new cab floor (the front being the end with the hole drilled in it) and place it in position with the hole over the 10BA nut and bolt.

When the glue has dried you can begin construction of the new bunker. First take the part of the old '1400' bunker with the buffer-beam attached and remove the bunker steps with a craft-knife, then file away any residue with emery-cloth. Now glue it to the new cab floor, ensuring that the rear buffer-beam aligns with the rear of the pony-truck, that the buffers are the correct height, and that the top and sides are square. When the glue has dried, fill the gap between the newly constructed bunker rear and the rest of the body with card or Plasticard. When the glue has dried, take the rear portion of the bunker top from the '1400' and glue it to the top of the section already in place, ensuring that it is square and level. Next glue the rear portion of the '1400' cab 3mm to the rear of its original position, ensuring that it is square and level with the rest of the body. When the glue has dried fill

the remaining gaps in the top of the bunker with card or Plasticard.

Now cut out a piece of paper 18mm x 71mm and glue it in place, wrapped around the rear of the bunker, to hide the joins. Then cut out two pieces of paper 8mm x 5mm and glue them in place, wrapped around the gaps in the tops of the cab doorways. Next take a 71mm length of 1mm-diameter wire, bend it to shape and glue it around the top of the bunker to form the top coal-rail. Camouflage the gaps in the running-plate on each side of the bottom of the bunker with pieces of 1mm-diameter wire. Now manufacture a new bunker top from card or Plasticard 29mm x 19mm and glue it in place 3mm below the top coal-rail.

Next manufacture a new cab front from card or Plasticard, using the old '1400' cab as a template for the radius of the roof (**Figure 7**). Offer the new cab front to the loco body and file away part of the '1400' cab front to align with the front spectacles. When this is done glue the new cab front in place. Now manufacture a new cab rear, using the same method as for the front (again **Figure 7**), and glue it in place. When the glue has dried, paint the inside of the cab.

From a piece of card 27mm x 34mm manufacture the cab roof, bend it to shape and glue in place. Next manufacture the roof-ribs from 1mm-square microstrip and glue them in place along the outside edges of the roof, together with a transverse rib at the halfway point. Then cut out a piece of card 10mm square and glue it to the cab roof just behind the front rib to represent the roof ventilator.

Glue the boiler and smokebox back in position and allow to dry. Cut out a piece of card 15mm x 25mm to form the top of the firebox, bend it to shape and glue it in place. Then glue a piece of paper 25mm x 21mm over the new firebox top to hide the joins and the 'threepenny-bit' effect. When the glue has dried, drill a 1mm-diameter hole through the top of the firebox 2mm from the cab front and 2mm to the right (fireman's side) of the centre-line. At this point it is a good idea to paint the bunker, cab and firebox with black gloss paint.

When the paint has dried glue a whistle into the hole drilled in the top of the firebox. I re-used one of the whistles from the '1400' – it is

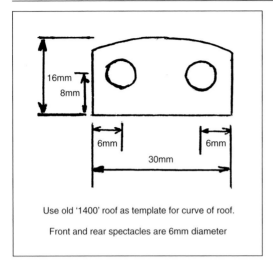

Use old '1400' roof as template for curve of roof.

Front and rear spectacles are 6mm diameter

Figure 7: New rear and front for cab

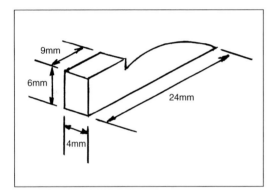

Figure 8: Combined splashers and sand-boxes

not an exact likeness of an LSWR whistle, but it's close. Next drill a 1mm-diameter hole through the top of each tank 1mm from the cab front and 2mm from the side of the firebox. Then take a 1mm-diameter piece of copper wire 3mm long (I used the copper piping from the Hornby 'Schools' 4-4-0 for this job), bend it to roughly match the curve of the firebox top and glue the ends into the holes drilled in the tops of the tanks.

Next manufacture combined front splashers

and sand-boxes from card or Plasticard (**Figure 8**), and glue them over the existing splashers.

We now turn our attention to the holes in the running-plate left by the removal of the splasher tool-boxes. Cut out two pieces of paper 18mm x 4mm and glue them over the holes. Next glue the replacement chimney in the same position as its GWR predecessor (I used a South-Eastern Finecast Drummond 'M7' chimney, from their 'M7' kit), ensuring that the chimney is straight and in line with the dome. Then fit the Ramsbottom safety-valves in position on top of the firebox, using photographs as a guide. There are quite a few manufacturers who produce these items, including South-Eastern Finecast, Westward, Craftsman and Alan Gibson.

Now drill a 1mm-diameter hole through each side of the boiler at its widest point, 4mm ahead of the front of each tank. Glue the clack-valves into each hole – good sources of clack-valves are South-Eastern Finecast, Craftsman and even Hornby (from the 'Schools').

You can now complete the painting of the body (gloss black, with the tops of the clack-valves in brass). Fit brass spectacle frames to the front of the cab – 6mm-diameter versions of these are available from Jackson-Evans and Mainly Trains. Similarly fit 6mm-diameter spectacle frames to the rear of the cab; these need to have 'coal-guards', and good sources are Craftsman and Mainly Trains. After fitting the rear spectacles, glue imitation coal on the top of the bunker, then fit lamp-brackets to the front and rear of the loco (SR locos had six at each end). The model is now ready for lining out and numbering.

According to my Ian Allan *Locoshed Book* of autumn 1961, the seven locos remaining in the mainland were Nos 30183/192/193/225 allocated to Plymouth (Friary), 30200/223 allocated to Eastleigh, and 30199 allocated to Salisbury. Of these, Nos 30183 and 30225 were 'push and pull'-fitted.

# Ex-SR '0395' 0-6-0 No 30567

The London & South-Western Railway's '0395' Class was introduced to service in 1881 and was designed by William Adams. The locomotives saw service on all parts of the South Western Division, from South West London to the 'Withered-Arm', and if your layout is in the latter territory one of these locos is a 'must'.

## Items required

Hornby 'Dean Goods' loco body and chassis; 4F tender and power unit; two Hornby GNR tender coal-rails; Hornby 'Schools' over-boiler copper steam-pipe; detailing parts as described in the text.

## Stage 1: The loco body

First of all separate the loco body from the chassis (they are held together by two screws, one at each end of the chassis). Then remove the cab with a penknife, but do not discard it. Next remove the lead weight from inside the boiler, held in place by a screw on the underside of the body, but again do not discard it. Now remove the top of the Belpaire firebox with a vertical cut immediately behind the fourth boiler-band, and two cuts angled downwards and outwards on either side of the firebox just below the boiler handrail (**Figure 1**). Be careful not to damage the boiler handrails.

Next remove the dome by filing away the plastic lugs on the inside of the boiler, then cut off the chimney and file any residue flush with the smokebox. Also file away the GWR lubricator pipe from the side of the smokebox, and any remains of the firebox top until it is flush with the top of the boiler. Fabricate a round-topped firebox from a piece of card 20mm x 35mm, bend

the card to fit the profile of the boiler and try in position. If it is too long, trim it until a satisfactory fit is obtained, then glue in place. When the glue has dried, take a piece of paper 20mm x 42mm and glue it over the new firebox top with each end just above the row of rivets at the bottom of the firebox – this will hide the joins and the 'threepenny-bit' effect (**Figure 2**).

Fill the recess left by the removal of the dome with filler, and when it has set file flush with the surface of the boiler. Next, with a penknife, remove the GWR vacuum-pipes and front sand-boxes. Remove the whistles from their sockets in the cab roof, then remove the plastic lugs from the underside of the cab. Remove the raised portion of the cab front (which fitted inside the Belpaire firebox) and file flush. Next remove the cab floor and the insides of the splashers from the underside of the cab and, with a hacksaw, cut the cab vertically in half.

Now manufacture a new 'full-width' cab front from a piece of card or Plasticard 30mm x 40mm (**Figure 3**). Cut 4mm-square slots for the rear splashers in the bottom edge, 3mm in from the outside edges. Next drill two 6mm-diameter holes 22mm from the bottom edge and 6mm in from the outside edges. Glue the two halves of the 'Dean Goods' cab to the new front with their outside edges in line with the outside edges of the new cab front. When the glue has dried, enlarge the windows of the 'Dean Goods' cab to the same size as the new cab front, then cut off the surplus material of the cab front above the roof-line of the 'Dean Goods' cab – follow the profile of the 'Dean Goods' roof (**Figure 3**).

Now offer the new cab to the loco body and test for a square fit with the running-plate and the rear of the firebox; if it is satisfactory, glue in place. When the glue has dried, fill in the gaps in

*Above* No 30566 was a member of the '496' Class, a variant of the '0395' 0-6-0s – note the square cab windows and longer front overhang. It is seen here at Eastleigh on 17 May 1953. *John Edgington*

*Below* The completed model of No 30567.

Figure 1: Removal of Belpaire firebox

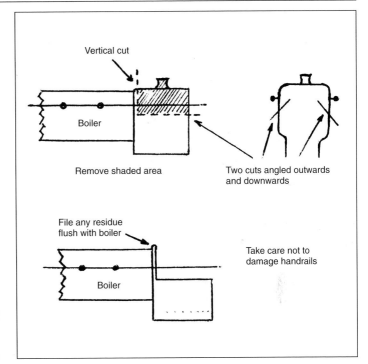

Vertical cut

Boiler

Remove shaded area

Two cuts angled outwards
and downwards

File any residue
flush with boiler

Boiler

Take care not to
damage handrails

*Below* Figure 2: Construction of round-topped firebox

*Below right* Figure 3: New cab front

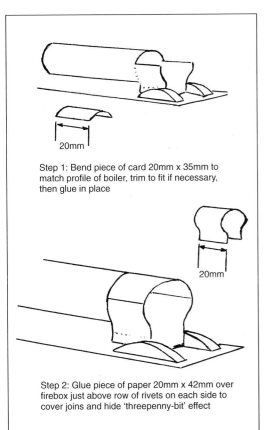

20mm

Step 1: Bend piece of card 20mm x 35mm to
match profile of boiler, trim to fit if necessary,
then glue in place

20mm

Step 2: Glue piece of paper 20mm x 42mm over
firebox just above row of rivets on each side to
cover joins and hide 'threepenny-bit' effect

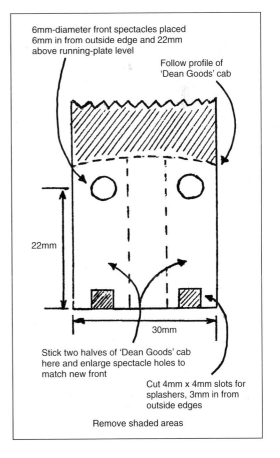

6mm-diameter front spectacles placed
6mm in from outside edge and 22mm
above running-plate level

Follow profile of
'Dean Goods' cab

22mm

30mm

Stick two halves of 'Dean Goods' cab
here and enlarge spectacle holes to
match new front

Cut 4mm x 4mm slots for
splashers, 3mm in from
outside edges

Remove shaded areas

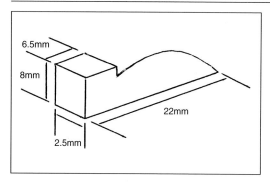

Figure 4: Combined splashers and sand-boxes

the cab front around the splashers, cab side-sheets and boiler backhead. When the filler has set, file flush with emery-cloth. Manufacture a new cab floor from card or Plasticard, 10mm x 18mm, and glue in place between the splashers.

Place the body on the chassis and check that the rear wheels are clear of the new floor and rotate freely. If not, trim the floor until it does clear the wheels. Next manufacture a new cab roof from card, 13mm x 33mm, bend to shape and glue in place, then make roof-ribs from 1mm-square microstrip and glue them to the outside edges of the roof, then add a centre transverse rib (use photographs as a guide). When the glue has dried, it is a good idea to give the cab and firebox a coat of black paint before fitting the detail parts. While the paint is drying, fabricate the combined sand-boxes and front splashers from card or Plasticard (**Figure 4**), and, when complete, glue them in place over the original front splashers.

Just before starting this project I was browsing through the Jackson-Evans catalogue and noticed that a pair of 6mm-diameter cab spectacles were available in etched brass. I ordered a pair and fitted them to the model; they come already cut out, so all you have to do is trim them and stick them in place – and very good they are too!

Next select a whistle for your model. I used an old Nu-Cast one left over from a kit, and glued it to the front of the cab slightly off-centre (the centre of the cab front will be occupied by the Ramsbottom safety-valves). Next we need a piece of copper pipe to fit over the firebox and supply steam to the whistle. I thought about using 1mm-diameter brass wire coated in copper

paint, but then I discovered the Hornby 'Schools' copper pipe, which I obtained from Modelspares of Burnley. Whichever method you use, use the photographs as a guide, and note that the bottom ends of the pipe follow the curve of the rear splasher. Next manufacture sand-box operating rods from 1mm-diameter wire, 63mm long, and glue them in place along the tops of the splashers (linking the front of the cab to the front sand-box) on each side of the locomotive (again, use the photographs as a guide).

All the photographs of '0395s' that I have seen show them with Ramsbottom safety-valves, and I obtained a very nice casting from Alan Gibson. I stuck that in the usual position and it looks very good indeed. As regards the Adams steam dome, I obtained that from Craftsman Models, and stuck it in the same position as its GWR predecessor. For the chimney, the Drummond 'M7' is the nearest I could find, and a very good white-metal casting is available from South-Eastern Finecast (from their 'M7' kit). Glue this in the same place as its GWR predecessor, and check that all three boiler mountings are square and in line.

Now for the clack-valves. I used a pair of Hornby 'Schools' valves obtained from Modelspares of Burnley, but a very nice pair of white-metal castings are available from Craftsman. Glue the clack-valves in place on each side of the boiler, just to the rear of the second boiler-band at the widest part of the boiler. Then manufacture a pair of cab handrails 7mm long, and glue them in place on each side of the locomotive in a horizontal position 16mm above the running-plate. Then give the body a final coat of paint, and it is now complete.

## Stage 2: The tender body

First separate the tender body from the underframe and power unit (held together by a screw on the underside at the front end of the chassis, and two plastic lugs). Then remove the brake handle and water-scoop handle for safe keeping. Next remove the top 5mm from each side and the water-dome, by drilling through from the top (**Figure 5**). I began with a 2mm drill and worked my way up in stages to a 10mm drill, which leaves a minimum of material to be

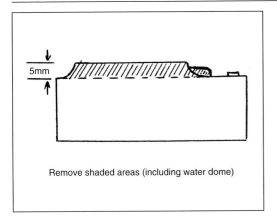

5mm

Remove shaded areas (including water dome)

Figure 5: Modification to the tender body

# Stage 3: The finishing touches

The only modification required to the loco chassis is the removal of the GWR outside brake-rodding – it is only a clip-fit, so a penknife should lift it off. The 4F and 'Dean Goods' have almost identical tender drawbars, so there should be no problem here. There shouldn't be too much difficulty in wiring up either; if you have wires attached to both loco chassis and power unit, simply splice them together and wrap them in insulation tape. If your power unit has had the wires removed completely, resort to soldering the loco leads to the terminals on the tender power-unit.

When you have completed the wiring, give the loco a road-test. If all is satisfactory, move on to the fine detailing, vacuum-pipes (as far as I know they were all fitted with vacuum-brakes), fire-irons on the tender, loco crew and lamp-brackets (Westward and South-Eastern Finecast do some particularly good ones). Note that the Southern used six brackets instead of the usual four.

Be careful when selecting an identity for your model. Some of these locos had square cab windows and a longer front overhang (see the photograph on page 82). The subject of my model, No 30567, was the last survivor of the class, not being withdrawn until late in 1959.

filed away. I did once try to drill through a piece of plastic with a 10mm drill without any pilot-holes, and it cracked the plastic! When the tender dome has been removed, cover the resulting hole with paper.

Clean up the top of the tender to take the coal-rails – I used the rails from the Hornby 'A3' (GNR tender). Make a 90° bend 13mm from the square end, then try in place. You will find that the lugs on the bottom of the coal-rails fit nicely inside the tender top. Ensure that the two sections of coal-rail meet at the rear of the tender, and when satisfied glue them in place. Finally replace the tender brake handle on the left-hand side of the tender footplate.

# Ex-SR 'C2X' 0-6-0 No 32545

Having been brought up in LNER territory, my first sight of a photograph of a double-domed 'C2X' came as quite a shock. Apparently this additional dome houses the top-feed, as favoured by a number of LMS and GWR designs; however, why do the 'C2Xs' have conventional clack-valves as well?

When D. E. Marsh became CME of the LB&SCR in 1905 he must have been unimpressed with the company's motive power, for he quickly set about rebuilding many of the existing designs. Witness all the classes that were rebuilt during his reign: 'A1', 'C2', 'D3', 'E1', 'E4', 'E5' and 'E6'. In 1908 the first member of Class 'C2' was rebuilt with a longer (superheated) boiler of increased diameter and was designated Class 'C2X' (the 'X' denoting a rebuild). These rebuilt locos must have been successful, for the rebuilding programme continued after the Grouping until 1940, when all 45 members of Class 'C2' had been rebuilt.

Despite the introduction of more modern designs after the Grouping (the 'Moguls', 'Qs' and 'Q1s'), all 45 'C2Xs' survived to become BR property in 1948. As far as I know they spent their entire careers allocated to LB&SCR (Central Division) sheds. The advent of the Birmingham RC&W Co Type 3s (later Class 33) in 1960 spelled the end for the half of the 'C2Xs' still in service, and they had all gone by the end of 1962, after a career of 54 years.

All the locos were fitted with Westinghouse pumps on the right-hand side of the firebox, some (*but not all*) had two domes, and some locos had Wainwright (SECR) smokebox doors (no doubt fitted after the Grouping), whereas others retained the original LB&SCR variety. All locos carried LB&SCR lamp-brackets, ie the two outer ones on the buffer-beam being longer than usual to carry two discs (one above the other), rather than the usual SR practice of two additional brackets on the front of the smokebox. The BR power classification was '3F', and most locos carried this above their cabside numbers. Some locos (but again, not all) were dual-braked, having vacuum brakes as well as Westinghouse; these locos had a vacuum ejector pipe fitted to the left-hand side of boiler together with *two* brake-pipes on each buffer-beam, so it is advisable to work from a photograph.

## Items required

Airfix, Dapol or Hornby LMS 4F; detailing parts as described in the text.

## Stage 1: The loco body

First of all separate the loco body from the chassis; it is held in place by two screws, one at each end of the chassis. Then remove the cab, which is only a 'clip-fit' and can be removed with a penknife blade. Next remove the smokebox door, boiler handrails, whistle and safety-valves. Also remove the regulator pipe (the plastic moulding on the left-hand side of the boiler), together with its associated pipework. Then remove the front vacuum-pipe, and the *leading* mechanical lubricator (the 'C2Xs' only had one). Next, with a craft-knife, remove the raised centre-part of the buffer-beam. Also remove the chimney and dome, and file any residue flush with the top of the boiler. Remove the lead weight from inside the boiler (it is held in place by two screws on the underside), and, with a hacksaw, remove the *rear* 11mm.

Next remove the top and rear of the Belpaire firebox (**Figure 1**). Be sure to leave the rear

Double-domed ‘C2X’ 0-6-0 No 32440 at Brighton on 5 October 1952. Note the Wainwright ex-SECR smokebox door.
*John Edgington*

*Below*  The completed model – I couldn’t resist making it one of the double-domed variety!

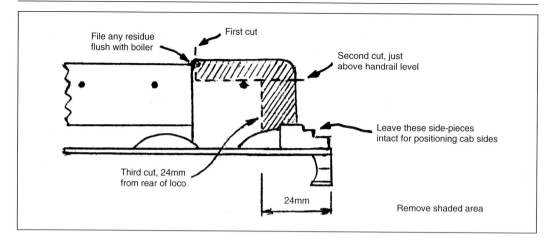

Figure 1: Modifications to firebox

splashers and the raised side-pieces of the footplate intact.

Using card or Plasticard, manufacture the front and sides of the new cab (**Figure 2**). When this task is complete (including the fitting of the cab-side handrails), glue the new front to the rear of what is left of the firebox, and ensure that it is straight and square. When satisfied, glue the new cab sides in position.

Fabricate a new top for the firebox from card, 17mm x 28mm, bend to shape and glue in place. Then cut out a piece of paper 17mm x 70mm and glue it to the underside of the firebox, and a second piece, 19mm x 68mm, trimmed at each end to fit around the rear and centre splashers. Try the paper in position over the outside of the firebox, then pierce holes in the paper so that it will fit over the rear handrail knobs. Glue the paper in position over the firebox, and it will hide the joins and the 'threepenny-bit' effect on the firebox top. Next fit a new boiler backhead inside the cab – a very good casting for one of these is available from South-Eastern Finecast (from their Wainwright Class 'C' kit).

Next drill three 1mm-diameter holes through the front of the running-plate, above the buffer-

Figure 2: New cab front and sides

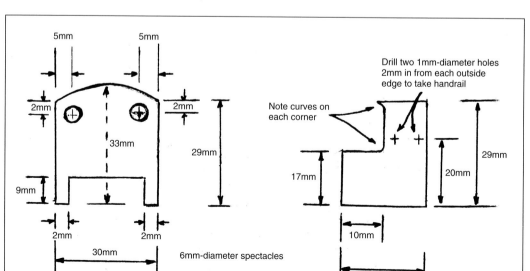

The front end of the loco showing the LB&SCR-pattern lamp-brackets.

beam, to take the lamp-brackets. Drill another 1mm-diameter hole through each side of the boiler, at its widest point, 10mm to the rear of the first boiler-band, to take the clack-valves.

Now we must turn our attention to the front of the smokebox. Take the moulding for the smokebox front of the 4F and, with a craft-knife, separate the door from the valve-chest cover with a circular cut following the curve of the smokebox door. With this done, glue the valve-chest cover back in its original position. At this point it is a good idea to fix the centre lamp-bracket in position – I always use the Westward variety on my models!

Now for the smokebox door, probably the most complicated part of the conversion. As I mentioned earlier, the 'C2X' Class carried two types of smokebox doors: the Wainwright SECR type, for which use a South-Eastern Finecast casting (from their SECR Class 'D' kit), and a standard LB&SCR door, for which you could use a South-Eastern Finecast casting (from their SR Class 'E2' kit) or one from the Hornby 'Saint' or

'2800' 2-8-0. The 'bulbous' profile of the last-mentioned item is spot on, although it is about 1mm too small in diameter. You could, at a pinch, re-use the 4F smokebox door – it is the correct diameter after all. With the removal of the LMS numberplate and the substitution of a smokebox dart in its place, and the removal of the 'dog clips' with a craft-knife, it would not be far off what it is supposed to be!

If you opt for the Wainwright version, the South-Eastern Finecast product is a very thin casting (approximately 1mm thick), so as we need to extend the smokebox by 4mm we need to cut 4mm from a 22mm-diameter broom-handle or 22mm-diameter plastic overflow pipe (whichever you happen to have to hand!). Alternatively you could fashion the smokebox extension from balsa. Once you have manufactured your smokebox extension, glue the Wainwright smokebox door to the front, having already fitted the handrail and dart – use photographs as a guide.

If you decide to use the South-Eastern Finecast 'E2' smokebox door, it will involve a lot of difficult work. The casting is 3mm thick and you will need to hollow out the centre of your smokebox extension to fit the casting into it! The two Hornby mouldings are a much easier proposition; that of the 'Saint'/'2800' already has a door-handle (dart) as part of the moulding, but no front handrail (re-use the handrail of the 4F).

The 4F smokebox door has no handle, so file away the numberplate and drill a 1.5mm-diameter hole to accommodate one – Markits and Jackson-Evans produce suitable items. It does, however, have a front handrail (albeit in the wrong place) – you could move it (using photographs as a guide) or leave it where it is, claiming 'modeller's licence'! The 4F smokebox door also has six 'dog clips' that will need to be removed, which is easily done with a craft-knife.

If you opt to use the Hornby mouldings, cut out a disc of thin card, 22mm in diameter, and glue it to the front of the smokebox. Then glue the 4F/'Saint' smokebox door to the card disc, having already carried out the modifications mentioned in the previous paragraph. Make sure that it is level and square, then cut out a thick piece of card 4mm wide by 67mm long and glue

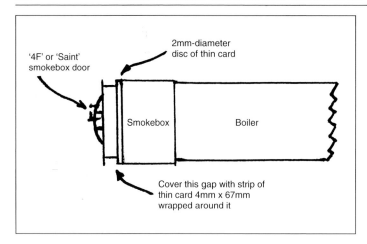

it in place, wrapped around the outside of the smokebox door (**Figure 3**).

Next fit the clack-valves, using photographs as a guide. I used the Markits SR clack-valves; while being very good quality and having plenty of copper piping with them, you need the eyesight of a hawk and three pairs of hands to assemble them! Next, from 1mm-diameter wire, manufacture the rear handrail for the cab. As this has to support the rear of the cab roof, construct it from a single piece of wire 85mm long; bend it to shape so that it matches the profile of the cab front, then glue it to the rear of the cab sides. From a piece of card 30mm long by 34mm wide, fashion the cab roof, bend it to shape, and glue it in place. It may be a good idea to hold the roof in place with rubber-bands while the glue is drying.

When the glue has dried, manufacture the roof-ribs from 1mm-square microstrip, one rib around the outside edge of the roof, and one transverse rib at exactly the halfway point (use photographs as a guide). Next replace the boiler handrails, then, depending on the identity of your model, fit a vacuum ejector pipe from a Hornby 'A3' 'Pacific'; at the time of writing these are still available from Modelspares of Burnley, but failing that a piece of 1mm-diameter wire will do the job (again, use photographs as a guide).

Now fit a Westinghouse pump to the right-hand side of the firebox; castings for these are available from many manufacturers. Then glue a short length of 1mm-diameter wire to the side of the firebox to link the front of the cab to the Westinghouse pump. Glue another short piece of wire from the leading side of the pump to disappear around the leading edge of the firebox (again use photographs as a guide). Next drill a 1mm-diameter hole through the top of the firebox, 1mm from the cab front and 3mm to the left of the centre-line, and fit the whistle (I re-used the 4F example).

Now fit the rest of the boiler mountings. All of mine came from South-Eastern Finecast; the Ramsbottom safety-valve casting is from their 'E2' kit, and is very nice! The chimney is from the 'I3' kit, and because of the extended smokebox it needs to be 2mm further forward than its LMS predecessor. As regards the dome(s), I used the castings from the Class 'Q' kit; if you are building a single-dome version it needs to be 2mm further forward than its LMS predecessor. If you choose the double-dome version, the rear one should be in the same position as its LMS predecessor, with the leading dome in line with the clack-valves. Finally ensure that all the boiler mountings are in line with one another. All the South-Eastern Finecast castings that I used on this model were of very high quality and are recommended.

Next fit the brake-pipe(s) to the buffer-beam – remember that if your model has a vacuum ejector pipe you will need two (dual-braked). Then fit the two outside lamp-brackets; the LB&SCR pattern were long enough to hold two discs, one above the other, so they need to be at least 8mm high! On my models I always use Westward lamp-brackets, and these include some long brass strips that can be cut to the required length (ideal for this job!). The loco-body is now ready for painting.

## Stage 2: The tender

First separate the body from the chassis and power unit – they are held together by a screw at the front end and a lug at the rear. Next remove the tender dome. I find that the easiest way of doing this is to drill it out – do it in stages up to 10mm (if you try to use the 10mm-diameter drill straight away you may split the plastic!). Then, with a craft-knife or hacksaw, remove part of the side-raves (**Figure 4**). Also remove the LMS-style fire-iron bracket from the top of the coal-space. Cover the hole left by the removal of the tender dome with a piece of paper. Using the craft-knife, alter the profile of the rear coal partition from a curved top to a flat one.

The 'C2Xs' had three coal-rails, which continued around the back of the coal space.

These can be made from 1mm-diameter wire or 1mm-square microstrip, and glued in place (use photographs as a guide). Remove the water-scoop handle (the left-hand 'brake handle') – there were no water troughs on the Southern. Next manufacture a couple of rear lamp-brackets from 1mm-square microstrip, 8mm in length, and glue them in place on the rear of the tender body. Add fire-irons to the right-hand side of the coal space – the Springside ones are particularly good. The tender body is now ready for painting.

The 'C2X' tender frames did not have longitudinal braces between the axle-boxes, whereas the 4F did. Therefore remove them with a craft-knife (**Figure 5**), and clean up any rough edges. If your model is to be one of the dual-braked locos it will need an extra brake-pipe on the tender buffer-beam (use photographs as a guide).

Your model is now ready for painting; the livery carried in BR days was unlined black.

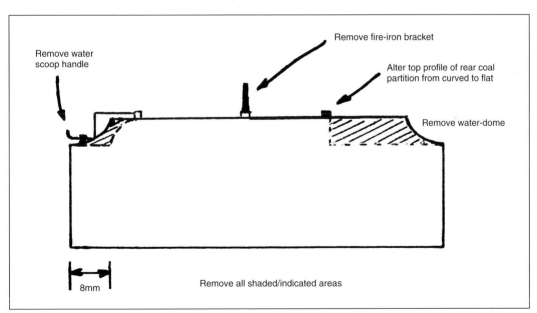

*Above* Figure 4: Modifications to tender body

*Right* Figure 5: Modifications to tender frame (springs omitted for clarity)

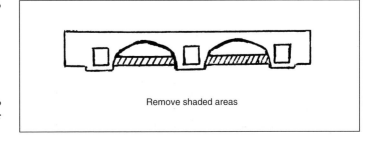

*Left and below left*  The completed tender showing the coal-rails and the modified framing.

*Below*  The rear of the tender showing the coal-rails wrapped around the rear of the coal space. Note the LB&SCR-pattern lamp-brackets (made from 1mm-square microstrip), and the *two* brake-pipes (No 32545 was dual-braked).

# SR PROPOSED 0-6-4T No 38002

**B**eing a Bulleid fan I have read many of the books on his career and products. In one of these books, *Bulleid of the Southern*, written by his son, I read about a design for a proposed tank locomotive that the Southern Railway toyed with in 1944. The intention was to replace the Class 'M7' 0-4-4 tank, a design that by then had been around for almost 50 years. The new proposal was effectively an 0-6-4 tank version of the 'Q1'. Unfortunately, while the Drawing Office team, the Operating Department and the Chief Civil Engineer all liked the design, Bulleid went off the idea and fancied something 'more modern'. So Bulleid and the design team set off on the road (or should we say cul-de-sac?) that led to the 'Leader'.

This was a great pity, for the 'Leader' episode greatly tarnished Bulleid's reputation and wasted thousands of pounds, which at the time (the middle to late 1940s) this country could ill afford. The 0-6-4 tank would have produced twice the power output of an 'M7' with a maximum axle-loading of 19.5 tons – more powerful, and lighter, than the 'Leader'. This surely was the correct road for Bulleid to have taken.

During my many years of reading *The Railway Modeller* magazine I have read articles by people who have built models of 'what might have been' – the GWR Collett 'Pacific' (a stretched 'King') and the GWR 2-10-2 tank (employing a 'King' boiler) immediately spring to mind – so why not dive into the realms of fantasy and build a 'might have been' of my own!

## Items required

Hornby 'Q1' (minus tender) – I managed to get hold of one that had been damaged in transit from China, which happens from time to time; front bogie from Hornby 'Merchant Navy'; detailing parts as described in the text.

## Interpreting the design

In the drawing (**Figure 1**) note that the bunker is almost identical to that of the LNER 'L1', and although no ladder is shown I am sure that Bulleid would have fitted one, as on the 'Q1s' and 'Pacifics'. According to the original drawing the bunker did not have additional water spaces, but if the loco had been built without them how would the fireman get to the top of the tanks to fill them? Therefore water-fillers at the rear of the bunker sides and equaliser pipes have been incorporated in the model. Note also that the boiler and smokebox are the same size, whereas on the 'Q1' the smokebox is smaller than the boiler. Would this feature remain at final building, or could the smokebox have reverted to the same size as the 'Q1' (in the interests of standardisation)? A case for 'modeller's licence' perhaps.

## Stage 1: The chassis

First remove the tender drawbar, retaining the fixing-screw for re-use. With wire-cutters (or even scissors) snip through the two pick-up wires, bind up their ends with insulating tape and tape them to the motor housing. Remove the rear section of plastic brake-rodding (**Figure 2**). Next, to permit the bogie to swing freely, the lower portion of the brake operating lever needs to be removed (again **Figure 2**). In addition, the rear metal bracket for the brake-rodding needs to be removed completely, *while at the same time leaving the drawbar fixing pillar intact*. This bracket

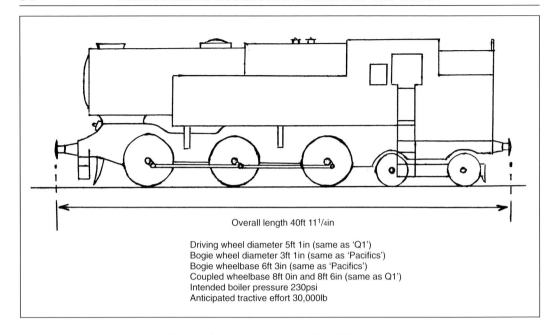

Overall length 40ft 11¼in

Driving wheel diameter 5ft 1in (same as 'Q1')
Bogie wheel diameter 3ft 1in (same as 'Pacifics')
Bogie wheelbase 6ft 3in (same as 'Pacifics')
Coupled wheelbase 8ft 0in and 8ft 6in (same as Q1')
Intended boiler pressure 230psi
Anticipated tractive effort 30,000lb

*Above*  Figure 1: The intended SR tank design numbered W.5975 and dated 27.9.1944

*Below*  The completed model of Bulleid's proposed 0-6-4 tank version of his 'Q1'.

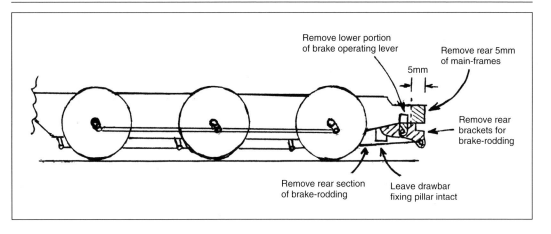

Remove lower portion
of brake operating lever

Remove rear 5mm
of main-frames

5mm

Remove rear
brackets for
brake-rodding

Remove rear section
of brake-rodding

Leave drawbar
fixing pillar intact

Figure 2: Modifications to loco chassis

is held in place by a small rivet located just in front of the pillar. I managed to remove the bracket with a pair of pliers, perseverance, and brute force. Then, with a hacksaw, remove the rear 5mm of the loco main-frames (again see **Figure 2**). With all of this work done, the bogie can now be fitted, utilising the tender drawbar fixing pillar and its associated screw. The chassis is now ready for road-testing.

## Stage 2: The bunker

First cut out a 20mm x 8mm piece of 1mm-thick Plasticard and glue it to the underside of the cab (**Figure 3**). Then cut out a piece of Plasticard or hardboard 43mm x 13mm and glue it to the underside of the cab, with its leading edge butting up against the frames, thus providing support for the new bunker (again see **Figure 3**). Next, from card or Plasticard, manufacture a floor for the cab and bunker 34mm long by 32mm wide, and glue it to the top of the bunker support immediately behind the original cab.

Again using card or Plasticard, manufacture the rear frame extensions (**Figure 4**), and glue them to each side of the bunker support with their rear edges in line with the rear edge of the bunker floor.

Fabricate the new cab rear (**Figure 5**) and the bunker rear (**Figure 6**) from card or Plasticard. Then cut out a rectangular piece of card or Plasticard 20mm x 17mm, and glue these three items to the cab and bunker floor (**Figure 7**).

Using a 1mm-thick piece of Plasticard,

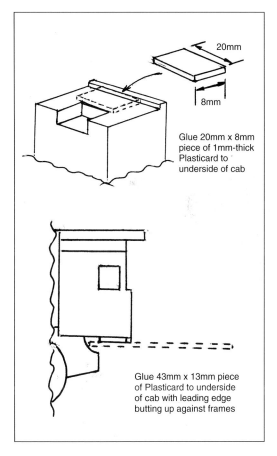

20mm

8mm

Glue 20mm x 8mm
piece of 1mm-thick
Plasticard to
underside of cab

Glue 43mm x 13mm piece
of Plasticard to underside
of cab with leading edge
butting up against frames

Figure 3: Underside of cab and bunker support

manufacture the rear buffer-beam, 33mm x 5mm. Then drill two 3mm-diameter holes on the centre-line, 5mm in from each outside edge, to take the buffers (**Figure 8**).

*Left* Figure 4: Rear frame extensions

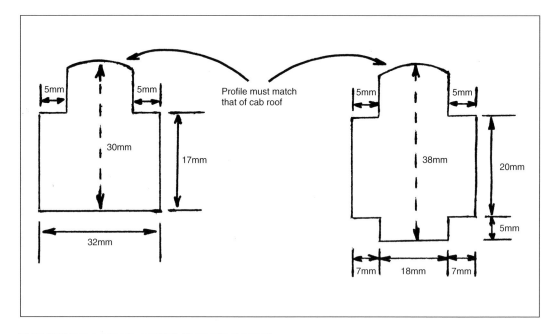

46mm

8mm

Curves must clear rear bogie wheels,
and will depend on layout track radii

5mm    5mm

Profile must match
that of cab roof

5mm    5mm

30mm

17mm

38mm

20mm

32mm

5mm

7mm   18mm   7mm

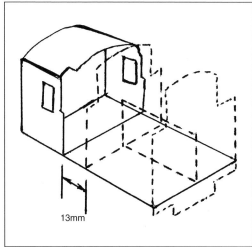

13mm

*Above* Figures 5 and 6: New cab rear and new bunker rear

*Left* Figure 7: Attaching rear of cab and bunker

*Below* Figure 8: Rear buffer-beam

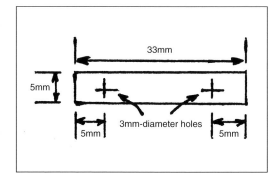

33mm

5mm

5mm

3mm-diameter holes

5mm

I used Cavendish sprung buffers (No 9 in their range) – they really are a very good product. Having fitted the buffers, it is time for the vacuum-pipe – I used one of the Romford wire-wound type (another product to be recommended). Once the buffer-beam is assembled (and the glue has dried) it can be attached to the rear of the bunker with its bottom edge level with that of the rear of the bunker.

Next manufacture the two bunker sides from card or Plasticard (**Figure 9**), and glue them in place with their bottom edges level with the top of the buffer-beam.

Use a piece of card 26mm x 12mm to form the extension to the cab roof. Bend it to the same profile as the roof and glue it in place between the rearmost edge of the roof and the top edge of the new cab rear. Then cut out another piece of card 34mm x 20mm to form the top of the

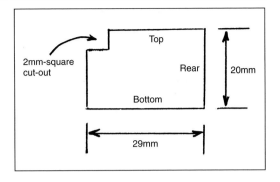

Figure 9: New bunker sides

bunker's bottom section, and glue it in place on top of the new bunker sides (**Figure 10**). Next cut out two pieces of card 13mm x 6mm to form the rear portions of the cab sides. Bend each to match the profile of the existing cab sides and glue them in place (again see **Figure 10**).

Figure 10: Assembly of bunker

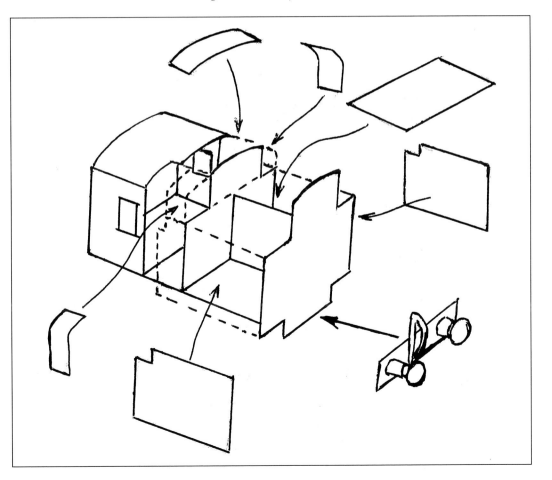

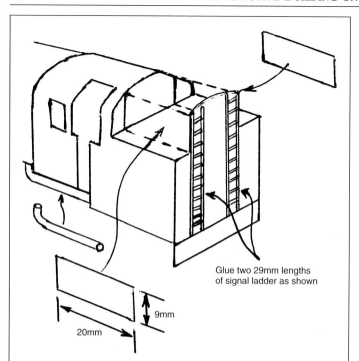

Figure 11: Assembly of bunker top

Glue two 29mm lengths
of signal ladder as shown

9mm

20mm

The rear end of the loco, showing the positioning of the SR lamp-brackets, made from 1mm-square microstrip, and the ladders, which are from Mainly Trains. Note also the circular tank-fillers.

Cut out two pieces of card or Plasticard 20mm x 9mm to form the sides for the top portion of the bunker, and glue them in place (**Figure 11**). Then cut out a piece of paper 28mm x 17mm and glue it over the top of the cab roof extension to hide and reinforce the join, and also hide the 'threepenny-bit' effect. Next glue two 29mm lengths of signal ladder to the rear of the bunker (also **Figure 11**). Plastic signal ladders are available from Ratio, while Mainly Trains produce some very good brass ones.

We now move on to the tank equalising pipes – while not shown on the original drawing I am sure that they would have been fitted. I used

35mm lengths of plastic sprue from a construction kit, with a suitable curve at one end. I glued them to the underside of the cab floor with one end disappearing under the bunker and the other disappearing under the firebox (**Figure 11** again). The pipe on the fireman's side required the removal of the injectors and under-cab pipework before it could be fitted! However, I was able to reinstate it all later while putting the tanks on – see Stage 3.

## Stage 3: The tanks

Figuring out how to construct the tanks took a while. The additional casing around the 'Q1' boiler only leaves a width of 3mm along the side of the firebox, with 4mm along the side of the boiler. I eventually hit on the idea of a Plasticard 'sandwich' – three layers of 1mm-thick Plasticard with an extra layer along the boiler. First cut out six pieces of 1mm-thick Plasticard 65mm x 17mm, and two pieces 25mm x 17mm, then glue the pieces together to make two 'sandwiches' (**Figure 12**). Having assembled the

two 'sandwiches', glue them to the sides of the loco with their bottom edges level with the bottom edges of the cab (**Figure 13**).

Next, in order to hide all the joins, cut out two pieces of paper as in **Figure 14**, and glue them to the bottom half of each cab side and each tank. Use PVA adhesive for this job as it is more 'forgiving' and allows plenty of 'slide'. Bend over and glue down the overlaps to cover the joins of the Plasticard 'sandwich'.

With the tanks completed we can now return to the under-cab pipework that we had to remove in order to fit the equalising pipes. To fix these in place I simply glued the tops of the pipework assembly to the inside of the bottom edge of the tank, together with a spot of glue to the inside of the injectors to glue them to the frames just below the equaliser pipe.

## Stage 4: The finishing touches

For the cab steps I used 14mm lengths of Plastruct laddering, and it does the job pretty

**Figure 12: Construction of Plasticard 'sandwiches'**

**Figure 13: Positioning of side tanks**

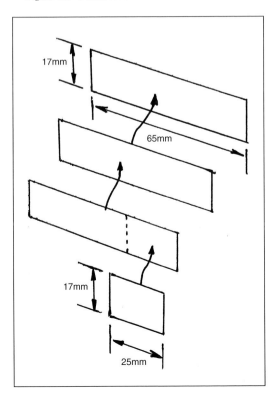

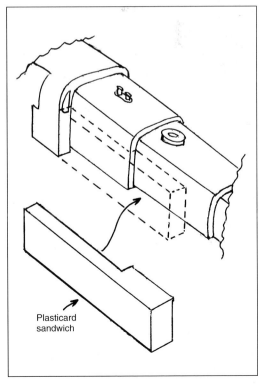

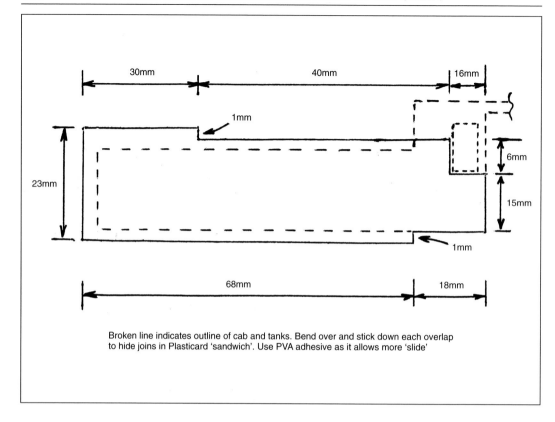

**Figure 14: Paper covers for side tanks**

well. While there are a number of white-metal castings on the market for water-filler covers, I preferred to use a couple of the white discs from the Hornby 'locomotive accessory packs' that usually come with each new Hornby loco nowadays (or available as spares from Modelspares of Burnley). I put one on the top of each bunker water tank at the rear corner. For the rear lamp-brackets I used six 5mm lengths of 1mm-square microstrip and glued them in the traditional places for SR locos.

When I had completed this model and I stood back to survey the result, I thought to myself what a beautiful engine – what a pity it wasn't built! This was certainly the road for Bulleid to have gone down rather than the 'Leader'. One final observation: in his book *Bulleid of the Southern*, H. A. V. Bulleid comments on the 0-6-4 tank design as, 'Probably the most unsatisfactory wheel arrangement in the history of steam engines.' All I can say is – my 0-6-4 runs very well indeed!

# Ex-LMS 5MT 2-6-0 No 42953

In 1933 the LMS introduced an updated version of its highly successful 'Crab' 2-6-0 design. The new class was designed by William A. Stanier, employed two outside cylinders with Walschaerts valve-gear, 5ft 6in-diameter driving wheels, and a modern tapered boiler. A total of 40 locos were built, and they all survived to become BR property in 1948. The first withdrawal did not take place until 1963, and the last was No 42954 in 1967. One member of the class (No 42968) has been preserved and can be seen on the Severn Valley Railway.

All members of the class were fitted with combined domes and top-feeds and ran with Fowler tenders. My 1959 Ian Allan *ABC* states that some locos were 'fitted with safety valves mounted on the top-feed', but I never saw one thus fitted! In BR days these locos were all allocated to London Midland Region sheds, but they did venture far afield on inter-regional freights (I remember a couple of occasions when one of the Aintree (27B)-allocated locos – Nos 42953 and 42956 – worked freights into Hull (West) marshalling yard in the spring of 1964.)

In OO gauge Millholme Models produced a white-metal kit for one of these locos, but it has been out of production for many years now. A model would certainly be something different, and would prove a useful addition to any London Midland Region layout, and possibly even some set in the North Eastern Region.

## Items required

Hornby Fowler 2-6-4 tank loco chassis (Margate version); Hornby 'Black Five' loco body; Bachmann Fowler tender or 4F tender kit; detailing parts as described in the text (including white-metal casting for 'Stanier combined dome

and top-feed', which as far as I know is only available from one source, Jackson-Evans, and as all members of the class had one you cannot build one without it!).

## Stage 1: The loco chassis

First detach the rear bogie from the 2-6-4T, then remove the rear 38mm of the chassis block with a vertical hacksaw cut. After cleaning up the sawn edges, replace the wheels of the pony-truck with a pair of 12mm diameter.

We now need to change the Fowler cylinders to a pair of the Stanier pattern. Comet Models manufactures a pack of parts (partly etched brass and some white-metal castings) to construct a pair of BR/LMS cylinders (as used in their loco kits). The pack – reference LC.01 – contains white-metal castings for the cylinder sides and valve-chests, with the front and rear of the cylinders on an etched brass fret. On my model I glued the sides and fronts over the existing cylinders (**Figure 1**), and as you can see from the photograph of the completed chassis the results are quite satisfactory. With this done your chassis is now complete and ready for road-testing.

## Stage 2: The loco body

For the construction of my model I used the body from a Margate-built tender-driven 'Black Five'. However, it should still be possible to use the body from the Chinese-built loco-driven version if you prefer. First remove the boiler handrails *and knobs* (they should lift off easily with the aid of a penknife blade) and put them aside for safe keeping; we shall be re-using them later. Next remove part of the fames from the underside of the loco directly beneath the smokebox (**Figure 2**).

*Above* Stanier 5MT 2-6-0 No 2971, still in LMS livery,
poses at Llandudno Junction shed on 25 April 1948. *John Edgington*

*Below* The finished model of BR-liveried No 42953.

The completed chassis – note the modified cylinders.

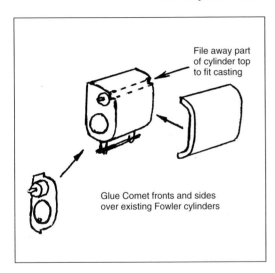

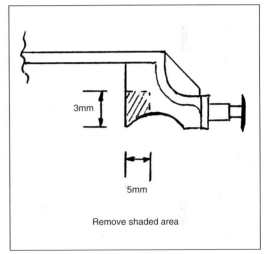

*Above*  Figure 1: Modification of cylinders

*Above right*  Figure 2: Modification to front frames

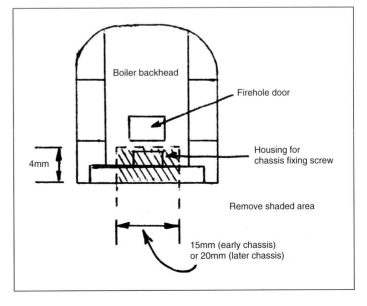

*Right*  Figure 3: Modifications to cab floor

We now have to cut away part of the cab floor to enable it to fit the rear of the chassis. The width of the cut may vary depending on the vintage of the chassis (early versions 15mm, later versions 20mm) (**Figure 3**).

Next, with a file or craft-knife, remove the leading sand-box fillers from both sides of the loco. Then remove the AWS cylinder from the right-hand running-plate. This is part of the body moulding and is difficult to remove – I drilled a hole through it, then filed away the rest. In order to shorten the body by 4mm, make two vertical hacksaw cuts through it as per **Figure 4**. Removing this section of the body will also take away the leading mechanical lubricator, but we still need to remove the remaining one with a file and/or craft-knife. Then, again with a file and/or craft-knife, remove the dome and top-feed, and file the remains flush with the boiler, *leaving the feed pipes intact* (also **Figure 4**).

After cleaning up the sawn edges of the two parts of the body, check for a straight and square fit and, when you are satisfied, glue the two parts together. Reinforce the join on the inside of the boiler with a piece of card; likewise reinforce the joins in the running-plate with strips of paper on both the top and bottom edges. When the glue

has dried, fill in any remaining gaps in the boiler join with Milliput or similar; likewise fill in the holes left by the removal of the dome, top-feed, mechanical lubricator and AWS cylinder. When the filler has set, clean off any surplus with emery-cloth.

Now a word or two about the reversing-rod. The Stanier 'Moguls' had one that was horizontal with a downward curve at the leading end (similar to the LNER 'B17'). Unfortunately the reversing-rod on the Margate-built 'Black Five' is part of the body moulding and its removal would mean a lot of hard work and would make a mess of the firebox side. In view of this I decided to invoke a bit of 'modeller's licence' and left the original in situ on the model. However, it would probably be a different story with the Chinese body, and the reversing-rod from a Hornby 'B17' would fit the bill (use photographs as a guide).

We can now press on with the fitting of the detailing parts. As I mentioned earlier, a casting for the 'Stanier combined dome and top-feed' is, as far as I know, only available from Jackson-Evans, and this goes *in the same position as the top-feed* of the 'Black Five'. In BR days all the class were fitted with AWS, and Comet Models

Figure 4: Modifications to 'Black Five' body

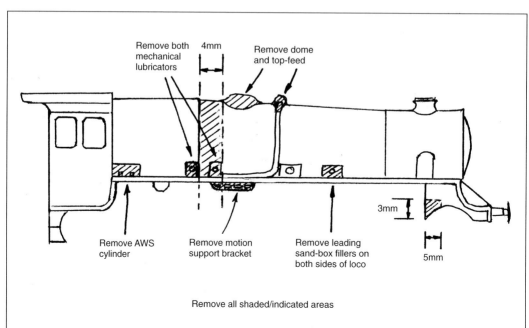

Remove both mechanical lubricators

4mm

Remove dome and top-feed

Remove AWS cylinder

Remove motion support bracket

Remove leading sand-box fillers on both sides of loco

3mm

5mm

Remove all shaded/indicated areas

produces a very good pack of white-metal castings for this equipment (reference LS.1 in their range). The pack contains a battery box, which goes on the right-hand running-plate immediately below the cab window, a large air cylinder, which sits on the running-plate approximately 4mm ahead of the battery-box, and a small cylinder, which sits transversely on the left-hand running-plate approximately 5mm ahead of the cab front.

Next, we need *two* LMS-pattern mechanical lubricators. Again, Comet Models produces very good castings for these (reference LS.40), while other possible sources are Alan Gibson, Jackson-Evans, and South-Eastern Finecast. These items go side-by-side on the right-hand running-plate, with the rearmost one 35mm from the front of the cab. Castings for the leading sand-box fillers are available from Craftsman Models (item No 95 in their range) and Jackson-Evans. These go on either side of the loco immediately behind the steam-pipes, in the angle where the smokebox meets the running-plate (use photographs as a guide).

Now drill three 1mm-diameter holes through the running-plate just above the buffer-beam to take the lamp-brackets. Westward and South-Eastern Finecast produce very good etched brass lamp-brackets. On this class the top lamp-bracket was positioned on the smokebox door just above the handrail (again, use photographs as a guide).

Fabricate a rear drag-beam from card or Plasticard 33mm x 8mm, and glue it to the rear of the cab with its bottom edge level with the bottom of the cab side-sheets. With this done, the more enterprising modeller may wish to insert a cab floor, seats, and even a loco crew (all a matter of taste!).

Next, from a sheet of 1mm-thick Plasticard cut out a rectangle 34mm x 12mm, and glue it to the underside of the body immediately beneath the steam-pipes. This will fill in the gap between the running-plate and the tops of the cylinders. All that now remains is the fitting of the boiler handrails, which will need to be shortened by 4mm, and the painting and lining. It would be advisable to apply the boiler-bands before fitting the boiler handrails. The livery carried in BR days was 'mixed-traffic', and the power classification was 5MT.

## Stage 3: The tender

The best source is the tender from a Bachmann 'Crab', and these do turn up as spares from time to time when the accompanying loco has been damaged in transit on its way from China. The only work this would need would be the fabrication of a drawbar to fit the pivot at the rear of the Fowler tank chassis (formerly used by the bogie swing-link).

Failing this, there are a number of kits on the market for an 'LMS Fowler 3,500-gallon tender'. Alan Gibson produces an all-brass kit with cast white-metal detailing parts, as do Comet Models and Jackson-Evans (both all-brass with white-metal castings). South-

The completed tender, based on the Hornby 4F version. Note the tender vents and the Craftsman Models coal-rails.

Eastern Finecast produces a kit with a white-metal body and a fold-up brass chassis. Needless to say, the white-metal castings included in the above kits are available separately from the manufacturers mentioned for those who wish to scratch-build.

It is also possible to obtain tender bodies from the Hornby 4F from Modelspares of Burnley and East Kent Models, so one could combine one of these bodies with a brass chassis from one of the kit manufacturers mentioned earlier. However, the tenders that ran behind the Stanier 'Moguls' differed from the Hornby/Dapol/Airfix model in having coal-rails, and tender vents at the rear of the tender adjacent to the dome (see the accompanying photograph). Sets of etched coal-rails are available from Alan Gibson, Jackson-Evans, South-Eastern Finecast and Craftsman Models. Likewise pairs of white-metal 'Stanier tender vents' are available from Alan Gibson, Comet Models and Jackson-Evans.

The tender attached to my model is a Hornby 4F tender with a burned-out motor! With the armature and initial gearing removed it runs very well, and the original drawbar couples up very well with the pivot at the rear of the loco chassis (previously used by the bogie swing-link). A pair of white-metal 'Stanier tender vents' from Comet Models and a set of etched-brass coal-rails from Craftsman Models completed the job.

# Ex-LMS (S&DJR) 7F 2-8-0 Nos 53808 and 53804

The Somerset Central Railway began operations in 1861, and a year later it renamed itself the Somerset & Dorset Railway. Its main line ran from Burnham-on-Sea to Broadstone Junction, where it connected with the London & South Western Railway (LSWR). In 1874 an extension was opened from Evercreech Junction to Bath (Green Park), thus making connection with the Midland Railway (MR). In November 1875 the MR and LSWR took over the operation of the line as a joint undertaking, and from then on it became the Somerset & Dorset Joint Railway (S&DJR).

While the LSWR was responsible for the supply of coaches and wagons, the MR looked after the supply of locomotives. The majority of S&DJR locomotives were therefore standard Derby products, eg 1P 0-4-4 tanks, 3F and 4F 0-6-0s, 2P and 3P 4-4-0s, and the ubiquitous 'Jinties', although Derby did produce one design specifically for the line – the 7F 2-8-0 designed by Sir Henry Fowler and introduced to service in 1914. It had 4ft 7½in-diameter driving wheels, a 4ft 9in-diameter boiler (as fitted to the Midland 'Compounds'), and two outside cylinders. Six locomotives were built, and because they were too long for the existing turntables on the S&DJR system it was anticipated that considerable tender-first running would be incurred; they were therefore equipped with cab-tenders (as fitted to the Lickey Incline banker, No 58100).

In 1925 a further batch of five 2-8-0s were supplied to the line, again designed by Sir Henry Fowler, but built by Robert Stephenson & Co of Darlington. This second batch differed from the original six in having 5ft 3in-diameter boilers and left-hand drive (the original six having right-hand drive). They also had standard Fowler 3,500-gallon tenders (ie without cabs),

the turntables on the S&DJR having been lengthened by this time. As a result, the original six locos began to lose their cab-tenders around this time. In 1930 the S&DJR loco fleet lost its separate identity and all of the locos were renumbered into the LMS fleet, and were re-painted into LMS livery.

In 1929 S&DJR loco No 89 (later BR No 53809), one of the large-boilered locos, was badly damaged in a collision. It was repaired at Derby and was returned to traffic with one of the smaller boilers, but it retained left-hand drive. S&DJR loco No 90 (later No 53810) was similarly rebuilt in 1930. However, the three remaining locos soldiered on with the original large boilers until well after nationalisation. No 53808 was re-boilered in 1953, 53807 in 1954, and 53806 in 1955, all with 4ft 9in-diameter left-hand drive boilers.

All 11 locos survived to become BR property in 1948 and became Nos 53800-05 (original six locos built with small boilers and right-hand drive), and 53806-10 (the five 1925-built locos with left-hand drive). Withdrawals began in 1959 with the condemning of No 53800, and were completed with the withdrawal of 53807 in October 1964. All 11 locos spent their entire careers allocated to Bath Green Park shed (71G/82F), although they made regular visits to Derby Works for overhaul and could afterwards be seen on 'running-in' turns in the Derby area. Thus one of these engines would be a useful addition to a Midland or S&DJR-based layout, while a South Western-based layout could just get away with having one.

The following model of No 53808 carries the larger boiler, while adaptations for a smaller-boilered version, No 53804, are given on page 119.

*Above*  The first of the initial batch of six smaller-boilered right-hand-drive 2-8-0s, No 53800, is seen at Bath Green Park shed on 29 June 1958. It became the first of the class to be withdrawn the following year. *Frank Hornby*

*Below*  The completed model of No 53804.

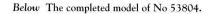

*Above* No 53808 was originally one of the 1925 large-boilered batch, but by the date of this photograph, 28 July 1962, it had been re-boilered with the smaller version. The location is again Bath Green Park. *John Edgington*

*Below* The model of No 53808 represents its pre-1953 large-boilered configuration.

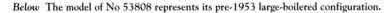

## Items required

Hornby (Margate) LMS 8F loco chassis; Hornby 'Patriot' loco body; Hornby/Dapol 4F loco cab; Hornby 'Patriot' tender; detailing parts as described in the text.

## Stage 1: The loco chassis and running-plate

First remove the 8F's 'firebox glow' assembly and retain the fixing screw for further use. Then, with a hacksaw and/or file, remove the raised portion of the chassis block that located the 'firebox glow' assembly (**Figure 1**).

We now move on to the cylinders. On the 7F they sloped at an angle of 12°, but on our model we cannot manage this (the 8F motion support bracket will not allow it). We can, however, raise the front of the cylinder block by a small amount to give a noticeable slope to the cylinders without the ends of the slidebars detaching themselves from the motion support brackets. Cut out a 10mm x 2mm piece of 1mm-thick Plasticard and glue it into the socket that holds the cylinder block at the front of the chassis, just ahead of the two raised lugs. This will raise the front of the cylinders by 1mm and will give a noticeable slope to the cylinders (see the accompanying photographs of the completed chassis). Then, with a craft-knife, remove the valve-chest tail-rods to permit the fitting of a new running-plate.

Figure 1: Modification to rear of chassis block

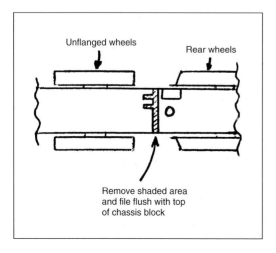

Unflanged wheels

Rear wheels

Remove shaded area and file flush with top of chassis block

From 80-thou Plasticard, manufacture a rear running-plate (**Figure 2**) and a front running-plate (**Figure 3**), then fix them to the chassis block with a 10BA nut and bolt (the front portion) and two 10BA screws (the rear portion); if you have retained the fixing screw from the 'firebox glow' assembly, it can be re-used as one of them.

We now move on to the raised portions of the running-plate above the cylinders. First cut out two pieces of 80-thou Plasticard 8mm x 3mm and glue them upright to the top of the front portion of the running-plate immediately in front of each cylinder (**Figure 4**). Then cut out two pieces of 1mm-thick Plasticard 8mm x 3mm and glue them flat to the top of the rear portion of the running-plate immediately to the rear of the cylinders (also **Figure 4**). Cut out two further pieces of 80-thou Plasticard 8mm x 32mm and glue them in place, bridging the gap between the two portions of running-plate (above the cylinders and combination-levers) (again see **Figure 4**).

Next, from card or Plasticard, manufacture the front frame extensions (**Figure 5**), and glue them to the inside edges of the raised sections of the running-plates. Note that their leading edges need to align with the front edge of the running-plate (use photographs as a guide). Next glue a mechanical lubricator into each of the holes that were earlier drilled through the rear running-plate (immediately to the rear of each raised portion). Comet Models produces very good white-metal castings for these (reference LS40 in their range).

Now cut out two rectangular pieces of card or Plasticard 36mm x 4mm to form the tops of the rear frames. Glue them to the running-plate lengthways, in line with the inside edges of each raised portion of the running-plate, and with their leading edges butting up against the rear edges of the raised portion of the running-plate (use the accompanying photograph as a guide).

## Stage 2: The loco body

The five locomotives introduced to service in 1925 were equipped with boilers of 5ft 3in diameter, and the Hornby 'Patriot' is a very good donor for boiler and firebox. The boiler diameter

*Right*  Figure 2: Rear portion of running-plate

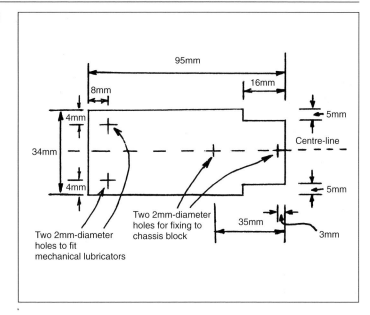

*Right*  Figure 3: Front portion of running-plate

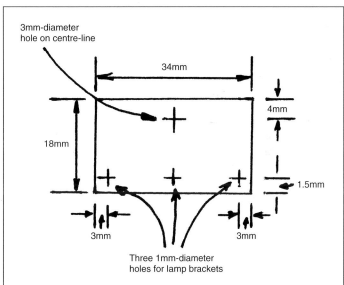

*Below*  The Hornby 8F chassis with the Plasticard running-plates fitted. Note the fixing nut and bolt and screws, and the packing piece that gives a slope to the cylinders.

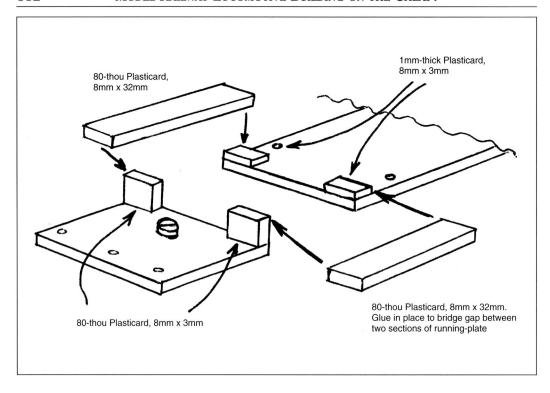

1mm-thick Plasticard, 8mm x 3mm

80-thou Plasticard, 8mm x 32mm

80-thou Plasticard, 8mm x 3mm

80-thou Plasticard, 8mm x 32mm. Glue in place to bridge gap between two sections of running-plate

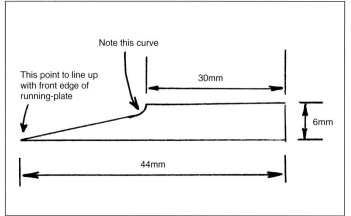

Note this curve

This point to line up with front edge of running-plate

30mm

6mm

44mm

*Above* Figure 4: Fitting raised portions of running plate

*Left* Figure 5: Front frame extensions

*Below* The chassis for No 53808 with completed running-plate. The mechanical lubricators, lamp-brackets, and front and rear frames are now in place.

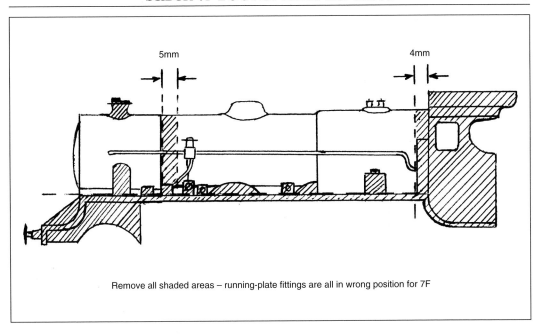

Remove all shaded areas – running-plate fittings are all in wrong position for 7F

**Figure 6: Modifications to 'Patriot' loco body**

is a scale 5ft 6in (a difference of 1mm in OO gauge), and being a Fowler product the firebox and dome are 'spot on'. Likewise the smokebox door is correct, although the more enterprising loco-builder may wish to replace the moulded front handrail.

First of all remove the chimney with a hacksaw, then remove the boiler handrails and retain them for re-use. Next make a vertical hacksaw cut through the firebox 4mm ahead of the cab front, then a horizontal cut along the upper surface of the running-plate (**Figure 6**). Using a craft-knife, remove the outside steam-pipes, splashers, sand-box fillers, mechanical lubricators, reversing rod, oil-boxes and rear sand-boxes (also **Figure 6**). We now need to shorten the boiler by 5mm. To achieve this make two vertical hacksaw cuts through the boiler, 5mm apart, between the rear of the smokebox and the vacuum ejector (again see **Figure 6**).

The vacuum ejectors fitted to both batches of S&DJR 7Fs were fitted *over* the boiler handrails on either the right-hand or left-hand side (as on the 4Fs – use photographs as a guide). Unfortunately the vacuum ejector on the 'Patriot' is an integral moulding 4mm below the left-hand boiler handrail. The easiest course of action would be to leave the moulding in situ and

invoke a bit of 'modeller's licence'; alternatively, the moulding and associated pipework could be removed with a craft-knife, and any residue filed flush with emery-cloth. A suitable plastic moulding from the Hornby 2-6-4 tank (Hornby reference L.5273) is available, at the time of writing, from East Kent Models and Modelspares of Burnley. Very nice white-metal castings for both left-hand *and* right-hand LMS vacuum ejectors are available from South-Eastern Finecast (from their 4F kit, which is available in both left-hand-drive and right-hand-drive versions). So, if you intend to remove the original vacuum ejector moulding, now is the time to do it, before you re-assemble the boiler!

Another job to be undertaken prior to re-assembling the boiler is the fitting of a new chimney. Alan Gibson produces a very good cast brass 'Austin Seven' chimney, which is very close to the required profile, and it needs to be positioned 15mm from the front of the smokebox. With that job done, you can then glue the smokebox and boiler together, reinforcing the join on the inside with a piece of card. Next glue a piece of card over the open end of the firebox – this will be used in due course for the fixing of the boiler backhead. Now cut out a piece of 80-thou Plasticard and glue it to the

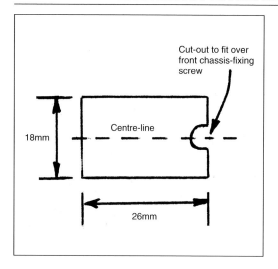

Cut-out to fit over front chassis-fixing screw

Centre-line

18mm

26mm

Figure 7: New base for smokebox

bottom of the smokebox (the circular cut-out at the front is designed to fit over the front chassis fixing-screw) (**Figure 7**).

Next drill a 1mm-diameter hole through the top of the firebox, 3mm from its rear edge and 3mm to the left of the centre-line, for the whistle. Fit the whistle and safety-valves – castings for these are available from many sources, and at the time of writing spare Hornby items are available from East Kent Models and Modelspares of Burnley.

We now turn our attention to the 4F cab. Spare Hornby 4F cabs are very difficult to come by – I just happened to have one left over from a previous conversion project. However, South Eastern Finecast produces a white-metal kit for a 4F, and it is possible to purchase the necessary castings for a 4F cab at a very reasonable price. On the front of the Hornby product are two raised sockets for fixing the boiler handrails; these need to be filed or cut away to allow a straight and square fit to the rear of the firebox. With that done, the cab can be glued to the firebox; use the four front windows as a guide to achieving the correct height and alignment. When the glue has dried and the cab is securely fixed, fit the boiler backhead in place; I used a casting from South-Eastern Finecast (again from their 4F kit), and, like all the rest of their products, the casting is of very good quality indeed. With the cab in place, fit the boiler handrails.

We can now move on to the vacuum ejector. At the time of writing a suitable plastic moulding (from the Hornby 2-6-4 tank, part reference L.5273) is available from East Kent Models and Modelspares of Burnley. This moulding is made to simply clip over the boiler handrail aft of the first boiler-band (use photographs as a guide to its positioning). If you cannot obtain the Hornby moulding, suitable white-metal castings are available from South-Eastern Finecast (again from their 4F kit). Unfortunately these castings are not made to fit over the boiler handrail, so part of the handrail would need to be removed to accommodate the casting.

Next, using Milliput or similar, fill in the locating holes for the 'Patriot' smoke deflectors, the holes in the sides of the firebox left after removal of the 'Patriot' sand-boxes, and the holes in the sides of the smokebox left by the removal of the outside steam-pipes. Just to the rear of the first boiler-band there are a couple of holes in the bottom of the boiler caused by the removal of the 'Patriot' mechanical lubricators, and these can also be filled, while at the same time fixing the front sand-box fillers. A set of four white-metal castings is available from Comet Models (from their 8F kit), and are of the correct size and pattern for our model. Simply push them into the Milliput filling at the base of the boiler 3mm to the rear of the first boiler-band; they need to be at a steep enough angle for the tops to protrude above the raised portion of the running-plate. You may need to make a lot of test fittings of boiler to running-plate before you get this right (again refer to photographs for guidance).

Next fit the lamp-brackets into the three holes drilled earlier through the front of the running-plate – I used Westward examples for the front of the loco. At this point it would be a good idea to paint the running-plate, the chimney, and the filled-in parts of the smokebox, boiler and firebox.

Next cut out two rectangular pieces of 80-thou Plasticard 20mm x 5mm and glue them to the bottom edges of the cab, then cut out two further pieces 5mm x 2mm and glue them to the front of the cab (**Figure 8**). With that done test-fit the boiler and cab to the chassis and running-

Figure 8: Making running-plate for underside of cab

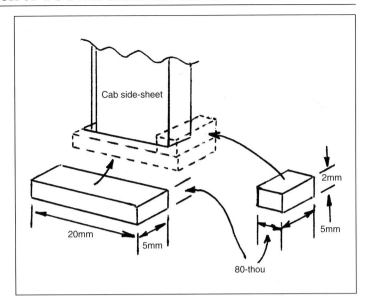

Figure 9: New front buffer-beam

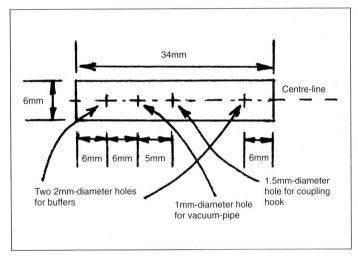

plate – hopefully the section of running-plate on the cab front will fit snugly under the main part of the main running-plate (it did on my model!).

Next manufacture the front buffer-beam from 80-thou Plasticard (**Figure 9**). I fitted Slaters sprung buffers to my model ('LMS standard pattern 16in diameter head', reference 4903 in their range) and a standard Romford vacuum-pipe, while the coupling hook came from Mainly Trains. When the buffer-beam is completed paint it red before gluing it to the underside of the leading edge of the front portion of the running-plate.

Fabricate a pair of rear sand-boxes from 80-thou Plasticard (**Figure 10**) – *make sure that the*

*hole for the filler is angled downwards* – then fit the Comet Models sand-fillers (from their 8F kit). In order to position the rear sand-boxes correctly, put the body in position on the running-plate before gluing them in place – they should butt up against the leading edge of the firebox, with their backs against the raised frames (again use photographs as a guide).

With the sand-boxes fitted in place we can now move on to the reversing-rod. On my model I used the example from the South-Eastern Finecast 4F kit, which is very close to the required pattern. Glue the rear end to the leading edge of the firebox, just above the rear sand-box (again use photographs as a guide).

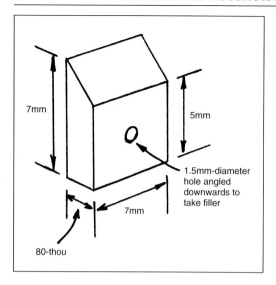

**Figure 10: Rear sand-boxes**

Next we need a pair of steps under the cab, and Jackson-Evans produces a set of white-metal castings for 'Stanier Tender Steps' that are ideal for our model; failing this the steps from the Hornby 'Patriot' could be used. Finally put a small spot of glue on the bottom of the nut and bolt holding the front section of the running-plate to the chassis block, to prevent them from working loose while the loco is in traffic.

# Stage 3: The tender

The tender from the Hornby 'Patriot' is an interesting creation – it has a lot of fine detail but is 4mm too long and 5mm too wide. One could use a bit of 'modeller's licence' and make do with the existing body, but is noticeably wider than the 4F cab! I decided to build a new tender body from card to achieve something closer to the required width, although there was nothing I could do about the length.

The Hornby plastic body is held in place by two lugs on each side of the tender frame, and these need to be cut or filed away. Then manufacture the new tender sides and rear from card (**Figure 11**). Pierce holes in the sides with a safety-pin to accommodate the handrails (**Figure 12**).

Next cut out a rectangular piece of card 30mm x 20mm and glue to the inside edges of the tender sides 7mm from the leading edges, thus

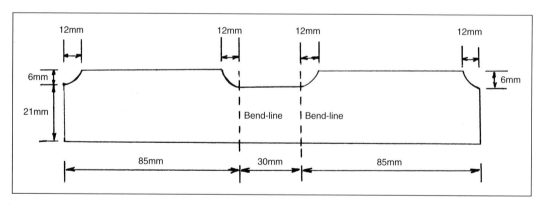

*Above* **Figure 11: Manufacture of new sides and rear for tender**

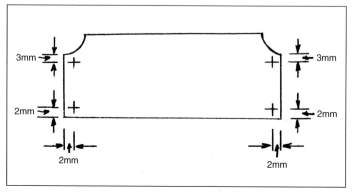

*Left* **Figure 12: Position of tender handrails**

forming the tender front. When the glue has dried, and we have a stable four-sided structure, fit the four handrails. The two front ones can be assembled in the conventional way with handrail knobs; however, the rear handrails will be too close to the rear weight to be able to use knobs. I just threaded the 0.7mm-diameter wire through the holes and bent over the ends on the inside with pliers.

The remainder of the tender construction is best carried out with the card body sitting in place over the mechanism. Cut out a rectangular piece of card 29mm x 20mm to form the top of the water tank. Pierce holes in the card to fit the dome and water filler as shown in **Figure 13**, and fit the two castings. White-metal castings for these two items are available from Comet Models and South-Eastern Finecast (from their 4F tender kits).

With the two castings in place, glue the tank top to the rear of the tender body with its underside resting on top of the rear weight. Then manufacture the two coal partitions (**Figure 14**), and glue them in position, the front one in the angles between the top edges and the front cut-outs (use photographs as a guide) and the rear one forming an angle of 90° with the top of the water tank.

Next cut out a rectangular piece of card 30mm x 5mm and glue it in place between the tender front and the front coal partition, thus forming a horizontal shelf. Then cut out a rectangular piece of 80-thou Plasticard 30mm x 9mm to form the footplate. Drill two 1mm-diameter holes (on the transverse centre-line) 4mm in from each outside edge to take the handles for the brake and water-scoop. White-metal castings for these are again available from Comet Models and South-Eastern Finecast (from their 4F tender kit). With these two castings fitted in place, glue the footplate in position at the front of the tender 5mm above the bottom edges. Next manufacture a top for the coal space, again from card (**Figure 15**). Pierce four holes through it to take the tender vents and fire-iron bracket; white-metal castings for the vents are available from Comet Models and Jackson-Evans, while a white-metal casting for the fire-iron bracket is available from South-Eastern Finecast. With the castings in place, glue the coal space top between the two coal partitions so as to cover the power-unit. When the glue has dried, cover the top with coal.

We now need a couple of steps on the rear of the tender. These can be made from rectangles of card or 1mm-thick Plasticard 2mm square and glued in place halfway up, 2mm in from the outside edge. Fine etched-brass lamp-brackets and etched-brass MR makers-plates are available from South-Eastern Finecast (from their 4F tender-kit). At this point the more enterprising loco-builder may wish to add more detail at the front end – lockers, coal-chute, fire-irons, etc.

The model is now ready for painting and

Figure 13: Top of water tank

Figure 14: Front and rear coal partitions

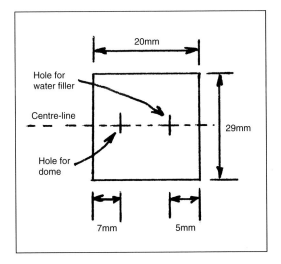

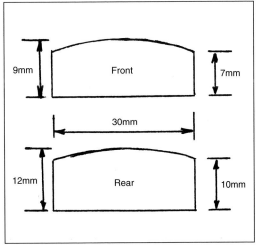

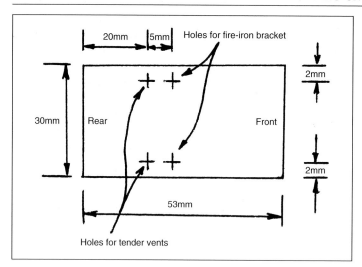

Figure 15: Top for coal space

The card tender body under construction: note the holes for the fitting of the handrails.

The completed tender.

application of transfers. The livery in BR days was unlined black, with the 'lion and unicycle' crest being the only style of BR crest carried while the locos had large boilers. Likewise, with a large boiler the only shedcode carried was 71G. The BR power classification was 7F and all locos carried this above the cabside numbers.

# No 53804: an interesting afterthought

Many years ago I constructed a couple of LNER 'J19s' utilising the chassis and running-plates from two Hornby 4Fs. This left me with *two* 4F boilers and cabs gathering dust in my scrap-box. Having used one of the cabs in the construction of No 53808, and encouraged by my success with that project, I decided to have a go at constructing one of the small-boilered 7Fs using the remaining 4F cab and the two boilers. I chose No 53804 for the identity of my model as it was one of the last two of the 1914 batch to be withdrawn (in February 1962).

To make the model, produce the modified 8F chassis in the same way as for No 53808, and construct the running-plate from 80-thou Plasticard in exactly the same way.

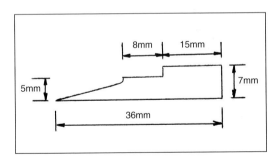

Figure 16: Front frame extensions for No 53804

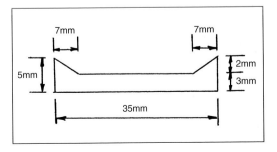

Figure 17: Rear frames for No 53804

The front frame extensions need a raised portion at the rear to represent the smokebox saddle (**Figure 16**). After gluing the extensions in place, glue a rectangular piece of card 20mm x 15mm between them, immediately to the rear of the front portion of the running-plate.

Next construct the rear frames from card or 1mm-thick Plasticard (**Figure 17**), and glue them in place along the rear portion of the running-plate, in line with the front frames, with their leading edges butting up against the rear of the raised portion of the running-plate (use photographs as a guide). Brace the rear ends of the frames with a rectangular piece of 1mm-thick Plasticard 15mm x 5mm glued between them.

As regards the sand-box fillers, Comet Models produces a set of very nice white-metal castings (from their 8F kit), although you need to manufacture your own rectangular mountings (9mm x 5mm) for the leading pair, which need to be glued to the inside edges of the raised portion of the running-plate (again see photographs as a guide). For mounting the rear pair of sand-box fillers I placed two 'blobs' of Milliput just inside the rear frames 8mm from their rear edges, then simply inserted the castings into the 'blobs' (see the accompanying photograph).

Remove the bottom portion of the 4F's smokebox front with a craft-knife (**Figure 18**). The bottom portion now becomes the front of the smokebox saddle and needs to be glued in place between the raised portions of the running-plate, while the smokebox door is now 'spot-on' for our model.

We now come to the most complicated part of this conversion: making the boiler and firebox from the 4F bodies. First remove the cabs and boiler handrails, then, using a hacksaw, cut up the two bodies as shown in **Figure 19**. After cleaning up the sawn edges with a file or emery-cloth, re-assemble four of the parts, again as shown in **Figure 19**. Reinforce the joins with card and fill in any gaps with Milliput or similar. The base of the firebox will need building up with layers of Plasticard or balsa, while the bottom of the smokebox will need filling with Milliput.

I replaced the Hornby 4F chimney with a

The chassis of No 53804 with partially completed running-plate: note the rear frames, mechanical lubricators and front and rear sand-box fillers, the latter set in the 'blobs' of Milliput.

The completed chassis and running-plate of No 53804: note the front frames and smokebox saddle.

white-metal casting for an 'LMS pattern 4F chimney' produced by South-Eastern Finecast (it goes in exactly the same position as its Hornby predecessor). I left the Hornby 4F dome in situ, and re-used the 4F safety-valves and whistle. The mechanical lubricators, buffer-

**Figure 18: Dissection of 4F smokebox front**

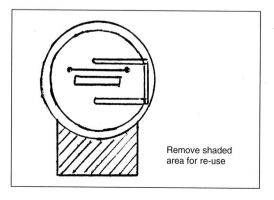

Remove shaded area for re-use

beam, cab steps and even the tender are the same as for the construction of No 53808.

The six locomotives built in 1914 were all right-hand drive, and remained so until final withdrawal. Thus the reversing-rod and the vacuum ejector need to go on the right-hand side of the loco. For my model I still used the South-Eastern Finecast reversing-rod, but the vacuum ejector involved a little more work. First the Hornby 4F vacuum ejector and its moulded pipework need to be removed, and the location hole filled in with Milliput or similar. As mentioned earlier, South-Eastern Finecast produces a kit for an LMS 4F that is available in both left-hand-drive and right-hand-drive versions, so they are able to supply both versions of vacuum ejector; unfortunately, while the casting is of very high quality, it is not made to fit over the boiler handrail, so I had to snip off the front 20mm of the right-hand handrail. That

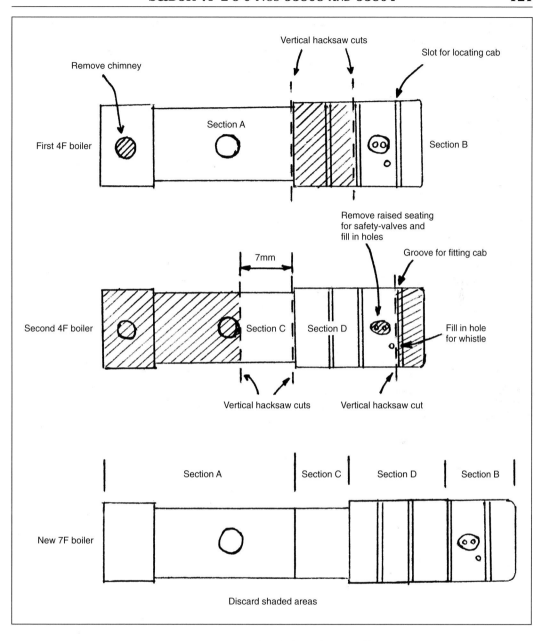

**Figure 19: Cutting of 4F bodies and re-assembly**

done, I drilled a 1mm-diameter hole (for locating the front of the casting) through the side of the smokebox 9mm from its leading edge, in line with the boiler handrail. After gluing the vacuum ejector in place, bend the vertical pipe to follow the contour of the boiler so that it disappears behind the frames. Then thread a small piece of wire through the front handrail knob and glue the rear of the wire to the leading edge of the vacuum ejector. With that done the model is ready for painting.

So if you find that you just happen to have two 4F boilers lying around gathering dust, I hope you will find this article useful. The photographs of the completed model demonstrate what can be done and, what's more, my models can negotiate second-radius curves and small-radius pointwork!

# Ex-GWR '2800' 2-8-0 No 3830

**M**any years ago Crownline produced an etched-brass kit to convert a Hornby '2800' 2-8-0 of 1903 into one of the '3800' series (sometimes referred to as the '2884' Class, as the 'modernised' 2-8-0s of 1938, with side-window cabs, etc, were numbered 2884-3866). Unfortunately Crownline is no longer in existence, but this need not be an obstacle to the enterprising loco-builder, for the necessary parts can be obtained from alternative sources.

A '3800'-series 2-8-0 would be a useful addition to any ex-GWR layout. The class survived until 1965 (the last full year of steam operation on the Western Region), and at the beginning of that year 22 were left in service: eight at Southall (81C): Nos 3812/18/20/48/51/54/59/66; five at Croes Newydd (84J): Nos 3813/17/49/50/55; six at Newport (Ebbw Junction) (86A): Nos 3808/30/37/40/61/64; and three at Severn Tunnel Junction (86E): Nos 3816/23/42. These 22 locos were all condemned during the course of 1965. (This information was obtained from *BR Steam Motive Power Depots: Western Region* by Paul Bolger, published by Ian Allan Ltd.)

## Items required

Complete Hornby '2800' loco and tender; cab from Hornby 'Castle' (at the time of writing this is available from Modelspares of Burnley, or the white-metal castings for a Class '2251' cab from South-Eastern Finecast could be used).

## Making the model

First remove the whistles, reversing-rod and boiler handrails from the '2800' loco body, and put them aside for re-use. Then remove the cab by making a horizontal hacksaw cut through the cab at floor level, and a vertical cut through the firebox 22mm from the rear of the loco (**Figure 1**).

Next, with a craft-knife, remove the boiler backhead from the remains of the '2800' cab and retain it for further use. In order to fit the 'Castle' cab over the '2800' cab floor we need to remove the vestiges of the cab side-sheets together with part of the cab floor – a total of 2mm on each side (**Figure 2**). Next remove 3mm from the bottom of the 'Castle' cab side-sheets (**Figure 3**).

Next, from thin card, manufacture a new cab front (**Figure 4**), and glue it to the front of the 'Castle' cab. When the glue has dried, glue the boiler backhead from the '2800' to the inside of the 'Castle' cab. That done, the cab can be glued in place.

When the glue has dried, fill in any gaps in the joins with Milliput or similar. Then drill two 1mm-diameter holes for the whistles through the top of the firebox 3mm from the front of the cab, and 2mm on either side of the centre-line.

**Figure 1: Removal of '2800' cab**

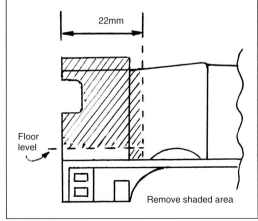

*Above* '2800' (or '2884') Class 2-8-0 No 3809 at Croes Newydd shed, Wrexham, on 20 September 1964. *W. G. Boyden, Frank Hornby collection*

*Below* The completed model of No 3830. The numberplates are by Guilplates, the 'Blue Spot' transfers by Fox Transfers, and the BR crests from Modelmasters.

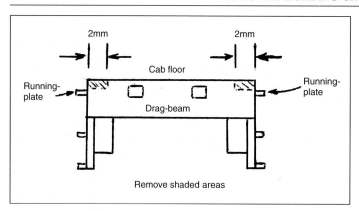

Figure 2: Modifications to cab floor to accommodate 'Castle' cab

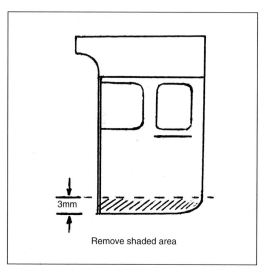

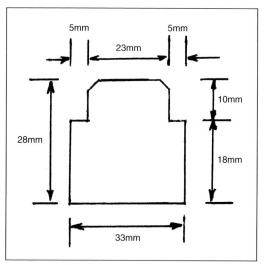

*Above left* Figure 3: Modification to 'Castle' cab

*Above* Figure 4: New cab front

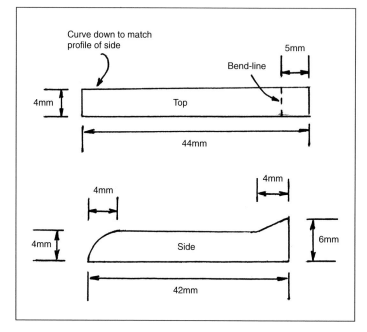

Figure 5: Making fire-iron box

Positioning the fire-iron box. The 'Blue Spot' transfer is by Fox Transfers and the numberplate by Guilplates.

Next, using card or Plasticard, manufacture the fire-iron box (**Figure 5**). Glue the two parts together, and when the glue has dried glue the 'box' to the *left-hand* side of the loco so as to cover the rear two splashers, with its rear end butting up against the front of the cab (use photographs as a guide).

The whistles can then be fitted into the holes made earlier in the top of the firebox. Then the reversing-rod and the boiler handrails can be refitted – note that, with the larger cab, these two items will need to be shortened by 6mm.

The model is now ready for painting and application of transfers. The livery carried in BR days was unlined black, and the route availability was 'Blue Spot'. Suitable numberplates are available from Modelmaster, CGW Nameplates and Guilplates, while transfers for Great Western route availability 'spots' are available from Fox Transfers.

No modifications are required to the loco chassis or tender, so your model is now complete and you have a useful and unusual addition to your layout.

# BR 204HP DIESEL SHUNTER No 11177

One day in the spring of 1960 I went on an engine-spotting expedition to Immingham with four friends from school. In those days Immingham was reached via a single-track branch-line from Goxhill and was not the 'Fort Knox' location that it became in later years. On our arrival we began to search for the shed, and one of our party reported that he had found a 'weird black thing' behind some tank wagons. The mystery item turned out to be Barclay 204hp 0-6-0 diesel shunter No 11177, one of two allocated to Immingham, and one of a class of ten introduced to service in 1956. Not long afterwards No 11177 was repainted green (with 'wasp' stripes) and was re-numbered D2400.

These ten locos spent unspectacular lives shunting at such glamorous locations as Immingham, Grimsby, Lincoln, Boston and Staveley. Withdrawals began in May 1967 with Nos D2406 and D2408, and continued steadily until January 1969, when the last three in service (Nos D2403, D2404 and D2407) were withdrawn. The last one to be cut up for scrap was No D2407 in August 1970. They were thus not a very large class, not very widespread and not very long-lived; but one would be something different on your layout!

## Items required

Hornby Class 06 diesel shunter body and metal frame (running-plate); Dapol 'Terrier' chassis; 35mm length of signal ladder (plastic or brass).

## Stage 1: The running-plate

First, with a hacksaw, remove part of the rear of the 06 running-plate so that it will clear the wheels of the 'Terrier' chassis (**Figure 1**). Next cut out a piece of 1mm-thick card or Plasticard 20mm x 18mm and glue it in place on the underside of the front of the running-plate between the front stanchions. Cut out another piece of the same material 22m x 8mm and glue it in place on the underside of the rear of the running-plate, making sure that it does not obstruct the holes for the cab fixing lugs (again see **Figure 1**). The running-plate should now fit the chassis, with the buffers at the correct height. Note that the *front* of the running-plate needs to go over the *rear* of the chassis.

## Stage 2: The body

The Class 06 body comprises a 'bonnet' section and a cab. The only modification required to the 'bonnet' section is the fitting of the signal ladder, bent to shape (use photographs as a guide), to the left-hand side of the body so that it leads up to the fuel-tank filler.

Next remove the glazing unit from the inside of the cab. This is probably the most difficult part of the conversion, but it is possible! Once done, remove the rear 3mm from the top part of the cab (**Figure 2**).

Clean up the sawn edges with a file or emery-cloth, then manufacture a new cab rear from thin card (**Figure 3**). Glue the new cab rear in place and fill in any gaps with Milliput or similar, filing away any excess. When the back of the cab was removed, the small electric headlamp moulding was lost, so manufacture a replacement from a piece of 1mm-square microstrip – this is fiddly but necessary – and glue it in place.

Next paint the cab, and when the paint has dried glaze the windows with clear plastic (having reduced the size of the cab we cannot re-

*Above* The Barclay 204hp diesel shunters would have become Class 05 under the TOPS scheme if any had survived long enough. This is No D2401, the former No 11178, at Colwick shed on 24 May 1964. It lasted until the end of 1968. *J. M. Tolson, Frank Hornby collection*

*Right* The completed model of No 11177.

use the Hornby glazing). With the glazing completed, paint the bonnet section, re-unite body and chassis, and add transfers and varnish. This model is something different, and the 'Terrier' mechanism performs much better than its Class 06 predecessor.

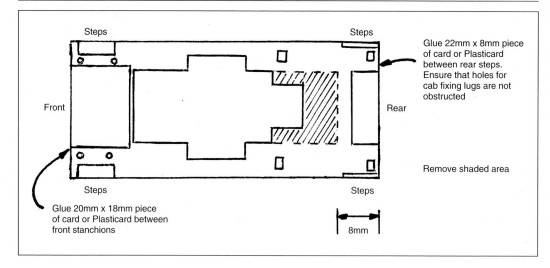

Steps                    Steps

Front                                              Rear

Steps                    Steps

Glue 20mm x 18mm piece
of card or Plasticard between
front stanchions

Glue 22mm x 8mm piece
of card or Plasticard
between rear steps.
Ensure that holes for
cab fixing lugs are not
obstructed

Remove shaded area

8mm

Figure 1: Modification to underside of 06 running-plate

Above  The modified running-plate and chassis assembled together.

Right  Figure 2: Modification to rear of cab

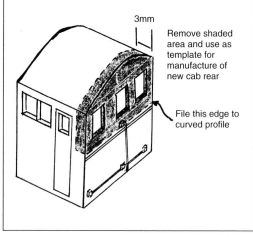

3mm

Remove shaded
area and use as
template for
manufacture of
new cab rear

File this edge to
curved profile

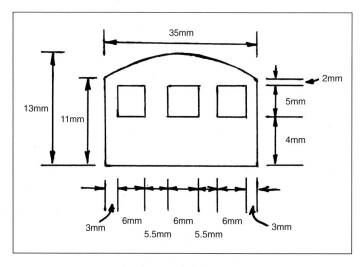

35mm

13mm

11mm

2mm

5mm

4mm

3mm      6mm      6mm      6mm    3mm
      5.5mm      5.5mm

Figure 3: New cab rear